Fighting Crime AND City Hall

The First Policewomen to Walk

A Beat in Indianapolis

By Patrick R. Pearsey

2018

Cover photo and design by David Dickens

From 1918-1922, the city of Indianapolis tried an experiment. They employed policewomen for the first time. They were an autonomous organization within the Indianapolis Police Department for several years, headed by an experienced social worker, Clara Burnside.

The experiment worked, by most accounts. Then, a new administration took control of city hall in 1922, along with the police department and things changed. This is an account of those years and the two dozen or so policewomen who for four years enforced the law their own way, without a gun.

I am blessed to work as the archivist for the current Indianapolis Metropolitan Police Department, with access to vintage photographs of the policewomen and the men they worked with and for. I was fortunate to receive the research on the early policewomen by the late Officer William Lichtenberger also. The files of the Indianapolis newspapers, the Star, News and Times are also primary sources.

Table of Contents

The Beginnings of Change

In April of 1891, the office of Police Matron was created by the Indianapolis Board of Safety. It was to be part of the Indianapolis Police Department. They appointed Miss Annie Mather to the position on April 8th.

Matron Annie Mather - 1896

Miss Mather received a room in the rear of the second floor of the station house on South Alabama Street to live in. She received a bedroom suite, donated by the ladies of the Meridian Women's Christian Temperance Union (W.C.T.U.).

Anna Mather was born December 22, 1845 in Newcastle-on-Tyne, England. She immigrated with her parents to the United States in 1854. They settled in a wooded part of Indianapolis. She received an education at School No. 8, on Virginia Avenue.

Her father took a job at the Indiana Women's Prison, where he was killed when a building under construction there fell. Her mother was then an invalid and Annie found a job in her teens, as a housekeeper at the Indiana Women's Prison.

She stayed there until 1886, when she became superintendent of the Home for Friendless Women in Louisville. She soon returned to Indianapolis to take a similar job at its Home for Friendless Women.

The Meridian W.C.T.U. had worked to get Annie Mather the position.

There had long been a need for a female matron to care for the needs of the female prisoners in Indianapolis. Annie Mather filled that need perfectly.

She was very busy, being the only person on the job, 24-hours a day, 7 days a week. In the Indianapolis Police Department's annual report on December 31, 1893, Annie Mather reported that she had 556 persons under her care during the year, including 510 girls and women, along with 46 boys under the age of 15.

Some of these women were taken to Central State Insane Asylum, the Home for Friendless Women and to the City Hospital.

The Superintendent in his report, praised the work of the Police Matron, saying, "No woman is so low, coarse, vulgar or filthy that the moment she is brought in the Matron is ready at any hour, be it day or night, to receive her, and when in proper frame of mind will hear from her words of comfort, cheer, and hope."

Annie was so successful in her position that the citizens of Indianapolis and of Indiana put forward a law enabling cities of ten thousand or more to provide Police Matrons at police station houses or jails to have charge of women and children while under arrest. This effort resulted in the passage of such a law in 1895. [1]

Annie found she had to resign due to the strain she was under from 6 years of constant work. She also was going to marry Wallace Logan, a railroad engineer.

Her resignation was accepted December 22, 1897. She was replaced by two police matrons, Mrs. Ella Gregorie and Miss Rena Reisner, at $50 a month, each.

Indianapolis Mayor Lew Shank offered these two women a position as detectives with the Indianapolis Police Department on August 15, 1911. The women talked to the Mayor but didn't feel he was entirely serious about the idea. They declined,

---

[1] Research notes of Officer William Lichtenberger, IPD.

saying they were well satisfied with their current positions as Police Matrons.

Mayor Shank's desire to hire policewomen became public and on November 15, 1911, City Hall was overrun with female applicants for the job of policewomen. They were camped out, young and old and continued coming throughout the day. This caught everyone, including the Mayor, by surprise.

Lieutenant John Corrigan, who talked to one ambitious young lady, said he didn't know of any positions open for either men or women. His understanding was that Mayor Shank's plan was only tentative and no money had been appropriated.

Only one woman managed to find her way to the Mayor. When he asked the lady to state her business, she replied, "I want a job on the police force."

"What qualifications do you have for the job? he asked.

"I've brought up three dear children and I brought them up right," she replied.

He suggested she come back when the matter was more definite.

Some of the women wanted to be detectives, having done that work for private agencies. Others felt they had the courage. Some women appeared at Police Headquarters to apply.

While this was going on, at a meeting of the Board of Public Safety that afternoon, Mayor Shank's suggestion to hire policewomen was not treated seriously and passed over in a light manner.

Mayor Shank was undeterred, vowing to bring two women with him to next week's board meeting, as well as some of the applicants for policewomen positions.

The final word, for now, came on January 3, 1912, from Superintendent of Police Martin Hyland. He appeared alone in the Odd Fellow Building and refused to appoint two policewomen to the police force.

Hyland stated he wanted 150 more men, but was granted only 20 and it was a "positive necessary each one should be a husky male."

Mrs. Grace Julian Clarke of the Local Council of Women told Hyland that two women in the twenty could do as much good as two men, their functions being to protect young girls on the streets and enforce the mashing ordinance, watching the picture shows, dance halls and skating rinks.

Apparently the Council of Women had two applicants prepared to join the force, if Hyland had been willing to appoint them.

Mrs. Alice Stebbings Wells, the first policewoman with the Los Angeles Police Department, paid a visit to Indianapolis in November 1912, as part of a speaking tour.

Members of the police force and public officials were invited to attend the meeting of the Women's Department Club when Mrs. Wells spoke and to meet her.

GRANTED POLICE POWERS HERE

MRS. IRENE V. WEBB

Another step forward to bringing women into law enforcement in Indianapolis came on December 5, 1912. Mrs. Irene V. (Jameson) Webb, age 69, financial secretary of the Indianapolis Humane Society, was granted special police powers by the Board of Public Safety.

She became the first woman in Indiana to hold police powers and this made national news. "Will you make arrests?" she was asked.

"I will if necessary," she replied, "but remember that I shall not seek opportunities to make arrests. I will use other means first."

Mayor Shank was responsible for Mrs. Webb being granted police powers. For 18-years she had been involved in the work of protecting children, first with the Indiana Children's Home, then for the last 18-months with the Indianapolis Humane Society.

It was her duty to go with the policemen on missions where the advice of a sympathetic woman was needed greatly (dealing with endangered children as they would now be called).

Former Indianapolis Police Matron Annie Logan became Indiana's first policewoman, on August 5, 1913, in the city of Madison. She did this for a year, resigning and returning to Indianapolis, on August 5, 1914. She had spent 40-years working in the areas of penal institutions and law enforcement.

The Indiana State House passed a bill which provided one policewoman to be appointed for every twenty men on the police force, February 16, 1916. This bill did not become law, however.

A Promise Kept

During the Mayoral campaign of 1917, Charles W. Jewett had made a promise to appoint female police officers to help combat vice in the city.

He kept this promise when elected. On March 23, 1918 he said "I promised that policewomen would be appointed to the local force. We now have several vacancies, but we intend to have several more." By that date, nine women had applied for the position of policewoman. Only one, Mary Egan, would be selected.

By law, each applicant had to be at least 35 years old and recommended in writing by no fewer than twenty women and five men, of whom had to have resided in Indianapolis for five years.

On May 8, 1918, the Board of Public Safety approved Mayor Jewett's recommendation to appoint 10 policewomen, making this a matter of certainty. There were over 50 applications for these positions on hand.

As these applications were reviewed the week of May 16, 1918, the applications would be ranked by a point system. Applicants would get points based on past experience, education for the position and ability.

The Board of Safety transferred $1,150 to cover the costs of furnishing and equipping the new policewomen's department at police headquarters.

City officials chose women who had some sort of background in nursing, social workers, as a jail matron, or who were known in the community.

Thirteen Policewomen Ready to Begin Their Work for City

Receive Badges From Chief Coffin After Appointment—Sergt. Clara Burnside in Charge.

Thirteen policewomen and a woman police sergeant were appointed to the Indianapolis police department at a special meeting of the board of public safety yesterday attended by Mayor Jewett, and Alexander L. Taggart, Felix Mc-Whirter and Henry Dithmer, members of the board.

Sergt. Clara Burnside, with the title of sergeant, will head the women's department of police and will be under jurisdiction of Chief of Police George V. Coffin. The other women appointed are Miss Sarah Osborne, 1102 Beville avenue; Mrs. Isabelle Phillips, 420 North LaSalle stret; Mrs. Clara Crooke, 3233 Ruckle street; Mrs. Irene Beyers, 1436 South Meridian street; Mrs. Bertha Duclus, 2957 Macpherson avenue; Miss Mary Egan, 1538 East Market street; Mrs. Anna Buck, 2926 Indianapolis avenue; Miss Rena Reisner, 2445 College avenue; Miss Elizabeth Whiteman, 430 North West street; Miss Lillian Jaschka, 28 South Alabama street; Mrs. Ella Gregoire, 2149 North Pennsylvania street; Mrs. Mary E. Mays, colored, 1043 North West street, and Mrs. Emma Baker, colored, 655 Blake street.

Miss Burnsides lives at 2110 Broadway, and in continued for the work of direct-

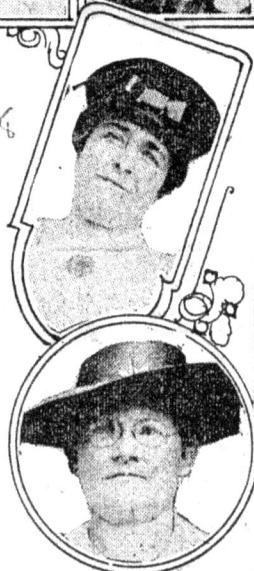

2

[22] IMPD Lichtenberger History Room.

18

At a special ceremony at City Hall on Saturday, June 15, 1918, fourteen carefully chosen women were appointed to the Indianapolis Police Department and given their badges.

To conform with the law, they were known that day as assistant police matrons but would be generally known as policewomen. After the appointments, the 14 women were introduced to Mayor Jewett and members of the Public Safety Board by Chief of Police George V. Coffin.

GEORGE V. COFFIN
Captain of Police

Mayor Charles W. Jewett, 1918 to 1922

Mayor Jewett said "I think that in the appointment of you women a great opportunity has been presented to the police department for a large amount of real constructive work. I know conditions as well as you do and I know there are a great number of young boys and girls in the city who need the proper kind of protection. If we can establish a safeguard for these young boys and girls, the assistance of the policewomen's department will be justified. I am proud to know that Indianapolis has taken this step for I know it is a step forward in the effort to suppress vice and immoral conditions."

The duties of the new policewomen, who would answer to a previously chosen Sergeant named Clara Burnside, were to combat shoplifting and the corruption of young girls and boys in Indianapolis. They would do this by frequenting arcades, Union Station and bars and taverns.

They were also to work as "Dance Matrons", keeping dancing from crossing over into what was then considered immoral behavior. That day, Chief Coffin explained to the women some of these duties. He said he was open to receive suggestions they might have about their work. Their first duty was to register aliens. He then presented them their badges.

The women, as described in the local newspaper that day, were:

Mrs. Mabel Phillips, who was in charge of the Indiana Girls School hospital for eight years. She had also been involved in social work.

Miss Lillian Jaschke, half-sister of the late Jake Kurtz, one of the best known detectives in the west. She had worked 3 years as a matron in the county jail.

Mrs. Bertha Duclus, who operated a grocery store with her husband. She was also a social service worker in the juvenile court.

Miss Mary Egan, a past probation officer in the city court and was now employed with the Charity Organization Society.

Miss Rena Reisner, police matron at IPD for the past 20-years.

Mrs. Ella Gregorie, police matron at IPD for the past 20-years.

Miss Elizabeth Whiteman, police matron at IPD for the past 8-years. Prior to this, she was matron at the county jail for 11-years.

Mrs. Irene Byers, widow of Lt. Byers of the Indianapolis Fire Department. Since his death, she had been employed in several downtown department stores.

Mrs. Clara Crook and Mrs. Anna Buck had served as social service workers in the juvenile court.

Mrs. Mary Mays served as a visiting nurse for the Flower Mission for 20-years. She also worked with the social service workers at the Indianapolis city dispensary. In addition, Mays had volunteered for 13-years in the juvenile court.

Mrs. Emma Baker had operated a laundry on Blake Street and was well known in the African-American community.

Photograph of the June 15, 1918 ceremony.

At this time, IPD had not selected a uniform for the women (and wouldn't, until 1922). They did wear the regulation policeman's badge, a six pointed star. Specially designed badges for them would be issued after their 90-day probation period.

Indianapolis Police badge style worn by Sergeant Clara Burnside

The women would work out of the second floor of Indianapolis Police headquarters.

This room had previously been used for the Identification & Records area.

Indianapolis Police Department Headquarters

The women reported to headquarters as instructed on Sunday afternoon. After walking up the stairs to their new office, they received an orientation provided by Captain Harry Franklin in the City Court room.

A former military man, he was responsible for instructing IPD officers on proper military conduct. The policewomen were then instructed by Lieutenant Reed and Lieutenant Claude F. Johnson in how to register the alien women. Albert Perrott, who brought the science of fingerprints to IPD in 1904, instructed them on how to take fingerprints.

Police Instructors of Policewomen

Lieutenant Claude F. Johnson

Top: Captain Harry Franklin.
Bottom: Albert Perrott

The women were instructed to report to Tomlinson Hall from June 17th to the 26th to conduct the registration of German alien women. They were also to report to police headquarters, 35 South Alabama Street the following afternoon to receive instructions for that work.

REGISTERING ALIEN WOMEN

"This picture was taken today, at Tomlinson Hall, where members of Indianapolis' new women police began the work of registering German alien women. The woman on the left of the picture is Mrs. Emma Baker, colored, one of the women police; next to her is one of the registrants; at the end of the table is Miss Clara Burnside, a supervisor of women police; at her left is another registrant and standing is Mrs. Clara Crooke, policewoman. "

After the registration work was done, all but three of the women were to be assigned to patrol public places in the downtown streets, in the public parks for supervision of girls.

Emma Baker and Mary Mays, the other African-American woman appointed that day, were assigned to patrol all of the neighborhoods in Indianapolis where African-Americans were predominating. Thus, they were segregated, as all African-American police officers had been with the IPD since 1876. They would receive the same salary as their white counterparts however.

By July, the work of registration of aliens was complete. On July 2, 1918, Captain Clara Burnside announced the new assignments for the policewomen. Police officers worked six days a week in those days.

IPD headquarters was abuzz on July 7, 1918 after two policewomen made their first arrest. Elizabeth Whitehead and Clara

Crooke arrested Alma Kriter, age 24 for vagrancy in Riverside Park. They weren't sure about the next step, so they phoned Sergeant Clara Burnside, who told them to have a patrol take the girl to police headquarters.

One thing needs to be said about the structure of the Indianapolis Police Department to understand how it operated until the 1970's. For decades up to 1918, the department basically changed hands every time city hall was taken over by a Democratic or Republican administration.

Each new mayor would appoint a Chief of Police of their own political party and then a patronage system of promotions would occur, which resulted in men belonging to the party out of power, being demoted for "inefficiency." This was common practice and would result in the hiring, promotion and demotion of policewomen in the future.

Indianapolis Police raided an apartment house at 410 North Alabama Street the evening of January 11, 1919. Lieutenant

Claude F. Johnson and a squad of police, along with Policewomen Elizabeth Whiteman and Irene Beyer arrested a girl and a 27-year old man. The pair was arrested on a morals charge.

The department's two African-American policewomen, Mary Mays and Emma Baker were involved in a series of investigations in 1919.

They saw a number of men thronging to a club at 525 Indiana Avenue in mid-February 1919. After seeing this for several nights they investigated on February 18th.

The women saw three women dancing, "cabaret style." They requested an opinion from Lieutenant William Cox and Sgt. John Volderauer. They arrived with a squad of policemen, watched the performance and arrested the three women on charges of vagrancy and disorderly conduct.

Policewomen Mays and Baker aided the IPD Morals Squad in a series of raids conducted throughout Indianapolis over the weekend of July 19-20, 1919. Twenty-nine people were arrested for illegal gambling or violation of the prohibition law.

Patrolman Harry W. Brooks

On one raid, Patrolmen Harry Brooks and Warren McClure, were carrying umbrellas, the policewomen carrying market baskets as part of their undercover disguise, evaded the watchful eyes of a lookout in front of Lew Harris' soft drink place at Indiana Avenue and Blake Street on July 19th. They aided the morals squad in raiding a crap game in a rear room.

Sergeant George L. Winkler

When two couples entered the place, the police dropped the umbrellas and rushed inside, grabbing the dice and money from a table. Sergeant George Winkler and Claude Worley, with several patrolmen, surrounded the place to prevent anyone from escaping.

Lew Harris was charged with keeping a gambling house and six others were arrested on gambling charges.

The team of Emma Baker and Mary Mays made another arrest on August 28, 1919. They were investigating a man who was getting children to sing and dance on downtown streets.

The arrest took place at Indiana Avenue and North Street. A crowd of about 500 people threatened Baker and Mays. They put in a call for assistance in a call box and Sergeant Maurice Murphy and an emergency squad arrived.

Photo of an IPD emergency squad.

A survey of moral conditions in Indianapolis by the Church Federation of Indianapolis resulted in a written statement issued October 11, 1919. In it, it commended the efforts of Jeremiah Kinney, chief of police and also commended the work of the policewomen of Indianapolis.

"The Federation also wishes to commend the work of the women police of Indianapolis. A long step has been taken in the interests of good morals in the appointment of these eleven women, who have given invaluable service to the city of Indianapolis during the last year."

The Board of Safety appointed two new policewomen on October 21, 1919, the first since the original appointments in 1918. They were Margaret Hildebrand and Mary K. Cantlon.

During the Christmas season of 1919, Indianapolis policewomen arrested 21 shoplifters – more than the total shoplifters caught by male officers in the last eight or ten years.

The women recovered approximately $500 worth of merchandise. Chief Jerry Kinney said he is well pleased with the work of the policewomen. "Keeping tabs on shoplifters is a work to which women are better adapted than male detectives."

Policewomen's Bureau - March 7, 1920.

---

[3] IMPD Lichtenberger History Room.

Policewomen were being paid $4.50 a day effective April 20, 1920, the same as their male counterparts.

Sergeant Charles J. Russell

The IPD Morals Squad conducted a raid of a suspected card game at 937 Massachusetts Avenue, July 29, 1920. At 4 p.m., Sergeant Charles Russell crept to the door of the apartment in question and heard enough to tell him gambling was going on.

He turned and winked at two policewomen who were with him. Russell tried the doorknob, which wouldn't turn. He stepped back and then crashed through the door with his shoulder and into a lively card party.

There were eight women around the table, who once they spotted the police officer, began screaming as they ran for other rooms, in a search for their hats.

Sergeant Russell had a big smile on his face and asked for the ladies to be calm as he called on the policewomen for help.

One lady ran for the door, blocked by the sergeant, pleading, "Oh, I just must get home. I haven't a minute to spare."

He said, "Very sorry madam, very, very sorry. But really you must spare just a few."

The eight women took their time to adjust their hats in preparation for the trip downtown in Sergeant Russell's car, all the while under the close observation of the policewomen.

"Whew, I'm glad these policewomen are along, Sergeant Russell said, seeing how they were taking a load off his back. The prisoners were also glad the policewomen were around. "I would just have died if the policewomen hadn't been along."

"They were awfully nice about helping us with our things when that awful man policeman told us we would have to go down to headquarters that is."

It took two trips to get the women to headquarters in the car, where they were booked and bonded out.

At the end of 1920, the case load of IPD's policewomen reached 4,120 cases, almost twice as many in 1919.

Officer Ruth McPhetridge

The appointment on March 2, 1921 of Helen Franke and Ruth McPhetridge as Indianapolis Policewomen brought the total number on IPD to 22. This gave the city more policewomen than any other in the United States. Washington D.C. had 20.

On April 23, 1921, *The Literary Digest* published an article about the Indianapolis Police Department's Department of Women, as it was then called. With 24 female officers, it was then known as the world's largest female police department.

[4] IMPD Lichtenberger History Room.

Clara K. Burnside was born December 23, 1874 in Indianapolis, Indiana to Thomas C. Burnside and Jennie O. Kelly. Her uncle was Ambrose E. Burnside, a Union General in the Civil War.

The family moved to Liberty, Indiana when Clara was a child. On the evening of May 20, 1892, Clara was one of seven graduates of Short High School in Liberty, Indiana. She delivered an essay to the crowd of one thousand people.

Clara left for DePauw University in Greencastle, Indiana that September. She was a member of Kappa Kappa Gamma sorority there and received a degree.

The first evidence of what became a life of public service for Clara Burnside came on January 3, 1901. She received an appointment as an instructor in the public schools of Puerto Rico.

Clara became employed as a Probation Officer for the Juvenile Court by May 1903. In August, 1906, she went to Puerto Rico to perform charity work. Going home for a visit, Clara boarded the S.S. Carolina on July 2, 1907 at San Juan, Puerto Rico, bound for New York City.

She arrived there July 7th. Clara was in Puerto Rico for three years, working with troubled juveniles. In 1909, she left Puerto Rico for Iowa. She returned to Indianapolis in January, 1910 and resumed her job as an investigating officer for the Juvenile Court, working with girls.

On September 19, 1911, the position of Chief Probation Officer for the Juvenile Court opened up and was offered to Clara.

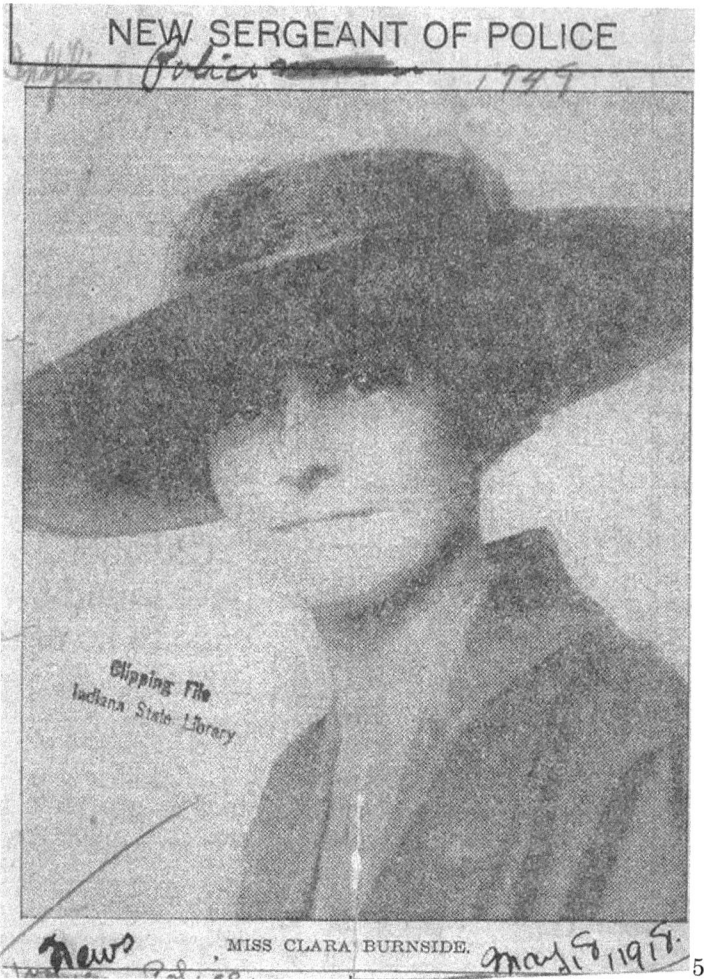

NEW SERGEANT OF POLICE

MISS CLARA BURNSIDE.

[5]

On May 18, 1918, Clara Burnside was
appointed the first woman police officer in
Indianapolis by Chief George V. Coffin. It
was announced at the time that she would
be the supervisor of women police, ten more

---

[5] IMPD Lichtenberger History Room.

to be named later by the chief. She would receive the rank and pay of a police sergeant.

Clara Burnside was endorsed by Frank J. Lahr, judge of the Juvenile Court, James A. Collins, judge of the criminal court, Alvah J. Rucker, prosecuting attorney, representatives of the Jewish federation, the board of children's guardians, the Mothers' Aid Society, the Children's Aid Society, the Public Health and Nursery Association, the Charity Organization Society and a number of leading citizens.

Clara was living at 2110 Broadway Avenue in Indianapolis at the time of her appointment.

The department of women would be a separate entity within the Indianapolis Police Department, with Sergeant Burnside answering directly to Chief Coffin. Coffin had this to say about Burnside's historic appointment:

"Miss Burnside, by reason of her long experience with juvenile court cases, fully understands the work she is about to take up and I am sure she will be able to conduct the women's department with a high degree of efficiency."

The women's department would occupy rooms then occupied by the police department's identification area on the second floor of headquarters.

Clara described her feelings about the appointment. "I am greatly interested in the work I am about to take up. The protection of young girls is a problem which demands a peculiar kind of knowledge and intuition which only women have, and I am sure the women's department will be able to make much progress in this kind of work. There is a big field to work in in Indianapolis and I am anxious to get started on it."

Thirteen carefully selected women were appointed on June 15, 1918 to work as policewomen. That day, all of them, along with Clara Burnside, received their badges and were sworn in as police officers.

Clara was an active police officer, not just an administrator. On July 10th, she and two of her policewomen, Elizabeth Whiteman and Clara Crook, arrested two men and two women at Riverside Park shortly before midnight. They were drinking brandy, which was against the Prohibition law at the time. They took them to police headquarters.

The policewomen of the Indianapolis Police Department were kept busy. On November 2, 1918 showed that the previous week, the 14 women handled 38 cases of girls, 20 women and three men. Three young girls were taken to the Juvenile Court, one man and one woman to the City Court and ten women were brought into the office of policewomen.

Clara Burnside's stated goal was to *not* arrest people if that could be avoided by counseling in her office.

Traction Terminal, Indianapolis, Ind.

Possibly the most dangerous day as a policewoman for Clara, came on December 29, 1918 near midnight. She was sent to the Traction Terminal Station to pick up all women they knew to be of questionable character. She left with Policewomen Rena Reisner and Bertha Duclus.

Burnside found numerous girls there that she felt were too young to be out so late, in the company of soldiers. The policewomen began taking them from the soldiers and sending them to their home or to the Detention Home. They took into custody one 17-year old girl, who was mentally slow. Soldiers made threats to the policewomen.

ALBERT RAY,
Sergeant of Police.

About 50 soldiers marched to police
headquarters and demanded the release of
the 17-year old girl. She wasn't in the City
jail upstairs and Captain Al Ray, who was
in charge, knew nothing about the case.
The soldiers returned to the Traction
Terminal station, where they found Clara
Burnside and her squad in a car ready to
start to their homes.

A group of soldiers surrounded them.
Policewomen at this time were not armed

with guns. Each time Clara started the automobile; the soldiers would jump on the running boards and "kill" the engine. They demanded the girl but were refused. They became so threatening that a riot call was sent to police headquarters on a Gamewell police call box.

Sergeant John Belch

A squad in charge of Lieutenant Johnson and Sergeant John Belch was sent and all of the patrolmen in adjoining districts were also sent to the Traction Terminal. Several patrolmen armed with heavy clubs were placed around it and remained all night.

Two male officers had similar trouble when they tried to take a girl from police headquarters to the Detention home. Their car was also surrounded by soldiers. Police said they had no trouble scattering the crowd in both incidents.

Clara attended the National Conference on Social Work & the meeting of the International Association of Policewomen, Atlantic City, New Jersey from May 31st to June 8, 1919.

One of the primary duties of the policewomen was to prevent shoplifting at downtown stores. They took this duty over from the detective division since they were so efficient at it. During the Christmas season, 1919, they arrested 21 shoplifters, according to Sergeant Burnside.

They also recovered $500 in merchandise. A number of other persons caught stealing articles from counters were released by the policewomen after a severe warning due to the small value of the articles taken. Chief Jerry Kinney said he was especially pleased with their work.

Clara was a frequent speaker at club meetings. At a meeting of the Women's Department Club, April 29, 1920, she said that training and trust alone is not enough for girls of 14 to 17 years of age. A girl who is 14 is not able to cope with the present world and that parents must give them some knowledge about problems with sex.

In June of 1920, Clara attended the national convention of the International Association of Police Chiefs, in Detroit, including a session on policewomen.

Clara Burnside was promoted to the rank of Lieutenant, July 13, 1920. She retained the title of supervisor of Policewomen. Clara was elected vice president of the State Association of Probation Officers and Police Women, November 15, 1920.

CLARA BURNSIDE
Supervisor   6

On March 22, 1921, the Board of Safety of
Indianapolis promoted Clara Burnside to
the rank of Captain. With her promotion,
the Indianapolis Star said that "this
department is placed at the head of similar

---

[6] Official IPD portrait, 1921.

organizations of the United States. In only two other cities are the women's departments under the supervision of a woman (Washington, D.C. and Seattle)."

They credited the success of IPD's Women's Police Bureau largely to Clara. There were now 23 policewomen, the most in the world according to one report this year. The women patrolled in pairs, six sets of women working from 2 p.m. to 1 a.m. The others were given general assignments and investigations.

Clara purchased a home and lot at 545 East 32nd Street in April 1921 for $8,250.

HEADS WOMEN'S POLICE FORCE

CAPTAIN CLARA BURNSIDE

May 1921

As she gave a speech to the National
Conference of Social Workers in Milwaukee,
June 23, 1921, Clara was described as the
only female captain of police in the United
States. She was then serving as secretary
of the International Association of
Policewomen.

On November 12, 1921, Clara Burnside, "chief of the women's police department of Indianapolis" resigned following an announcement by Samuel Shank, mayor-elect, that the women police would not operate as a separate department and that most of the women would be put in uniform.

Chief Jeremiah Kinney

When she submitted her resignation to Jerry Kinney, chief of police, she asked that it become effective January 1st.

Women's Police Chief Quits Over Uniform

MISS CLARA BURNSIDE.

Special to The Courier-Journal.

INDIANAPOLIS, Nov. 19.—Wear uniforms, Mr. Shank?

Emphatically no, replies Miss Clara Burnside, chief of the Indianapolis women police to the Mayor elect and forthwith turns in her resignation.

Which proves, critics of the Mayor-elect say, that men should not try to pick clothes for women.

And they add that his order is practicularly unfortunate in this case because Miss Burnside's department has been pointed to as a model all over the country. Not long ago the Literary Digest published an article on the department.

Often the women police go to the homes of girls to confer with parents. Since they do not wear uniforms none know of these visits except members of the immediate families.

Mayor Shank requested John W. Mullin on December 12th, to ask Clara Burnside to remain with the police department. Mullin said he wanted to have her and Policewomen Bertha Duclus, Irene Beyer and Nell W. Dunkle become members of the detective department with the rank of detective sergeant.

Mayor Shank wanted two more women to join the detective department. Clara agreed to this. She was demoted to Sergeant, January 2, 1922 so she could take charge of female investigators in the Juvenile Court.

Clara was a principal speaker at a dedication ceremony of a newly completed women's department at the Marion County Jail, April 1, 1922. It was also the one hundredth anniversary of the founding of Marion County.

Clara Burnside on October 31, 1922 handed her resignation from IPD to Chief Rikhoff and asked it take effect November 1st. She was resigning to accept a position as adult probation officer of juvenile court. Stating she had a desire to return to the juvenile court, she said "My relations with Chief Rikhoff have been most cordial. I have no complaint at all to offer as to his treatment of me."

She began working as a probation officer for the Juvenile Court of Marion County. On June 22, 1923, she attended the executive board of the Family Welfare Society. She declared that the society could do much to assist the court by reducing the number of cases coming before it. The society was determined to investigate moral conditions in theaters and parks as pertained to Indianapolis youth.

Clara was promoted to Case Supervisor of the Juvenile Court on October 3, 1923.

On May 19, 1928, Clara Burnside died of tuberculosis in Indianapolis. She was described by Judge Frank J. Lahr of Juvenile Court at her death as the most capable woman in Juvenile work in the country. The Indianapolis Star described her as known nationally as one of the pioneers in juvenile court work. She had been sick seven weeks and in ill health for over a year.

She is buried in West Point Cemetery, Liberty, Union County, Indiana.

[7]

Mary A. Egan was born May 6, 1866 in County Cork, Ireland to Jeremiah and Hanora (Irwin) Egan. This family originated in Carragane of County Cork.

---

[7] Official IPD portrait.

In 1869, Jeremiah Egan took his family to the United States and settled in Indianapolis, Indiana. The family is found living in Indianapolis, Indiana in the 1880 U.S. Census. Jeremiah Egan was a gardner. Mary, aged 14, was then in school. They lived at 729 East Market Street.

The father died in 1903. The remaining family including Mary lived at 1559 East Market Street, 1910. Mary Egan was then working as a clerk in a furniture store. Mary Egan was appointed as a Police Court Matron, January 25, 1914 on the recommendation of Chief Samuel Perrott.

A number of prominent club women signed a petition for the appointment of Miss Egan. She also served as probation officer for the court. She remaining there through 1918. On March 11, 1918, she was appointed a Police Matron.

Mary had been doing charity work. These facts made her attractive to the Indianapolis Board of Safety when they were searching for suitable candidates for policewoman in 1918.

Mary was living at 1538 East Market Street when she was appointed a policewoman. Her first assignment was to help register German aliens at Tomlinson Hall on June 17, 1918. She received her permanent assignment July 2, 1918. She was to conduct special investigations in police headquarters, 8 a.m. to 6 p.m.

On September 12th, IPD detectives were closing in on Ned Williams, who had committed his 13th robbery. They found and arrested him that day. He told them that he was afraid the shock of finding out he was arrested would prove too much of a shock to his ill wife, so policewoman Mary Egan was called.

Egan said later that the wife thought her husband was working for an industrial concern. During the month of October, 1918, Mary investigated 29 complaints, nineteen girls and ten women.

During the investigation of a surgeon performing illegal operations, Mary Egan and Detective George Hanks took the statement of a 17-year old girl, which led to his arrest on June 22, 1920.

Promoted

LIEUT. CLARA BURNSIDE AND SERGT. MARY A. EGAN.

On July 13, 1920, Mary Egan was promoted to the rank of Sergeant, the 2nd highest ranking policewoman on the department. She was the assistant of Captain Clara Burnside. She was promoted to the rank of Lieutenant of policewomen on June 14, 1921.

With the election of Mayor Louis Shank, six policewomen were chosen to serve in the Detective Department with the title of Detective on December 15, 1921. One of these was Mary Egan. However, Mary Egan turned in her resignation to the Board of Safety on January 3, 1922.

Mary A. Egan, age 54, died May 14, 1926 of arterioscierosis in St. Vincent's hospital, Indianapolis. She is buried in Holy Cross Cemetery.

Police Matrons
Clockwise from top middle,
Mary Egan, Elizabeth Whiteman,
Rena Reisner & Ella Gregoire. All
became policewomen, 1918.

Anna May (Wells) Buck was born October 20, 1866 in Illinois to Wilson D. Wells and Meranda Coleman. Her family moved to Indianapolis in 1873. Anna attended School No. 41 on Rader Street, between 30th and 35th Streets.

She married Cassius C. Buck in 1886. They resided in Indianapolis, 1900. They lived at 1212 25th Street. Cassius was a carpenter. In 1910 they resided at 824 31st Street.

They had four children, Helen, who died as an infant; Elsie E., Clifford C., a WWI veteran and Theodore A. Buck, who died at age 10.

Her husband Cassius was a chronic alcoholic who couldn't quit drinking. While on a binge, he was standing with Anna in the kitchen. While she had her back turned, he shot himself with a revolver, committing suicide.

Anna Buck was a member of the suffragist movement in Indiana. The movement in the United States formed "leagues" and when the North Indianapolis League formed in early 1915, Anna was elected treasurer.

She attended the Woman's Party convention in Chicago, June 5-7, 1916. She served as chairman of the suffrage committee.

Among the resolutions that came out of this convention was to vote against the Democratic nominee, whose party had been opposed to the passage of a national suffrage amendment and to vote support

the Republican presidential candidate,
Charles Evans Hughes.

Opening session of the Women's Party
convention, June 5, 1916.

Indianapolis Suffragists Active in Chicago.

ALTHOUGH INDIANA IS NOT A SUFFRAGE state its women are taking an active part in all the suffrage meetings in Chicago this week and the state is represented in the woman's party convention called by the Congressional Union. Among those who are attending from Indianapolis are Miss Eleanor P. Barker, Mrs. Caroline B. Curtis, Mrs. Ida Gray Scott, Mrs. F. R. Wands, Mrs. Anna Buck and Mrs. A. W. Cobb and Mrs. R. E. Hickman.

MRS. CAROLINE B. CURTIS. MRS. IDA GRAY SCOTT.

MRS. ANNA BUCK BRETZMAN PHOTO

The Congressional Union organized the
Fourth Ward Club at Anna's home,
September 15, 1916. Mrs. Buck served as

chairman. This meeting was geared toward the suffrage movement.

She continued with the suffrage struggle, presiding over a meeting of the Women's Party, April 6, 1917.

Anna became one of the first policewomen in Indianapolis, June 15, 1918. Issued badge number 3, she then lived at 2926 Indianapolis Avenue. She had volunteered as a social service worker in the juvenile court previously.

Anna and Policewoman Irene Beyer were assigned to patrol motion picture houses, department stores and other public places in the downtown district, July 2nd, 1:30 p.m. to 11:30 p.m. Anna Buck joined Bertha Duclus and Rena Reisner in patrolling the Transit Terminal Station and Union Station when movie houses were closed, in October 1918.

When policewomen were assigned by Mayor Shank to do individual patrols (without a partner as was the practice), Anna Buck was assigned to Union Station. She reported first to police headquarters on January 5, 1922, for 7 a.m. roll call and then was sent to Union Station by Captain Walter White.

Anna Buck personnel record.

Captain Walter White

On Friday, the 13th of January, 1922, Policewoman Anna Buck reported for roll call and was told by Captain Walter White that she had been assigned to a beat.

Her new hours would be the same as the male officers, 7 a.m. to 8 p.m. She had been working 7 a.m. to 3 p.m. at Union Station.

Captain White said this was an order from Chief Rikhoff. Anna Buck wondered about the choice of the 13th having any significance.

She was assigned to District number 23, bounded by New York, Noble, Alabama and St. Clair Streets. She went out and inspected her district, then went home.

On March 16, 1922, Anna was one of six policewomen detailed to different schools to protect children leaving school and walking through traffic. Anna was sent to Public School 49 at Morris and Kappes Streets.

On February 22, 1923, she was assigned to collect fines in the City Clerk's Office. After being sent to watch a film "The Slave Mart", on July 6, 1923, Anna Buck filed a report to Captain John White, who ordered scenes cut from the film.

Anna Buck - 1921

One of the duties of policewomen in the 1920's was to serve as Dance Matron. Anna Buck in 1924 was assigned to this duty, watching the dance floor intently to make

---

[8] Official IPD portrait, 1921, IMPD Lichtenberger History Room.

sure the dancers didn't do anything indecent (by 1920's standards). Non-policewomen Dance Matrons were still paid by the City of Indianapolis until 1968. The annual salary of Anna Buck in 1925 was $1,733.50.

Policewoman Anna Yoh

Policewomen Anna Buck and Anna (Peats) Yoh were walking along Illinois Street, just south of Washington Street on September 3, 1926. They saw a young man, later identified as Chalmers Valentine, accost a young woman and grab her arm.

They asked the girl if she knew the man and she said she didn't. The told him he was under arrest. He jerked loose from the policewomen and ran across Illinois Street, with the women in "hot pursuit", or as the *Indianapolis News* described the next few moments:

"Racing madly through downtown streets, and alleys, with two fleet-footed policewomen right on his heels, a young man Thursday night learned it is futile to attempt an escape from the feminine minions of the law, unless one is equipped with a racing car. The youth came out loser in the exciting foot race and landed in the hoosegow."

The chase wound through Pearl Street, Meridian Street, Maryland Street, back to Illinois Street, 10 seconds ahead of the policewomen. The man finally ducked into the Hotel Severin coffee shop. The policewomen followed, along with a city fireman.

The chase continued out the coffee shop, through the hotel lobby and down into the basement until in an elevator, the exhausted, panting, youth was apprehended. The fireman subdued him but he surrendered to Anna Buck and Anna Peats. The youth said he thought he knew the woman on the street.

Anna was assigned as a jail matron in late 1926. By February 1928, she was working for the missing person's department of IPD.

Anna attended a suffrage committee reunion on September 13, 1928, so she kept in contact with the women who helped get the vote for all women.

The Board of Safety retired Anna Buck from the force on November 13, 1928 because she was found unfit for further duty by the police physician.

Anna Buck sued the city for back pay on February 27, 1929. The suit stated that she was dropped from the city payroll on November 15, 1928, although no charges had been filed against her. She continued to report for duty, following notice of her dismissal, but that Chief of Police Claude M. Worley refused to assign her to duty.

Policewoman Anna Buck

Chief Claude M. Worley

Anna demanded $496 due her. She was being paid $164 a month when dismissed. Chief Worley said "She is not on the police pension roll because she was past the age limit requirement for admittance to the fund provisions when she was appointed to the force." Anna was 51 when appointed in 1918 and 62 when dismissed from IPD.

Anna Buck filed another lawsuit on March 30, 1932, asking for $6,500 in salary due her since being pensioned off. Anna Buck died of heart disease on February 16, 1933 at her home, 836 West 31st Street. She was a charter member of the St. Paul M.E. Church and a member of the International Travel and Study Club. She was buried in Crown Hill Cemetery, Indianapolis, Indiana.

Service revolver of Policewoman Anna Buck. Photograph courtesy of Stacey Foley.

A New Administration

Mayor Lew Shank

During the electoral campaign for Mayor of Indianapolis in 1921, Republican candidate Samuel Lewis "Lew" Shank made a number of statements that were disturbing to policewomen. Among these were that if elected Mayor, he wanted them to wear uniforms. Their preference was to remain in plain clothes since that was how they arrested shoplifters.

He also said he would eliminate the current Department of Policewomen and fold them into the body of the department.

Finally, he stated that if a woman's police department was maintained, that it should have a working force of women past middle age. Current Chief of Police Jerry Kinney allowed that while some members might be rather young for their work, he found them entirely competent. He had never had a complaint concerning them.

Lew Shank received petitions bearing the names of thousands of women in favor of the present organization of policewomen.

On December 15th, Mayor-elect Shank announced his plans to choose six policewomen were chosen to serve in the Detective Department with the title of Detective.

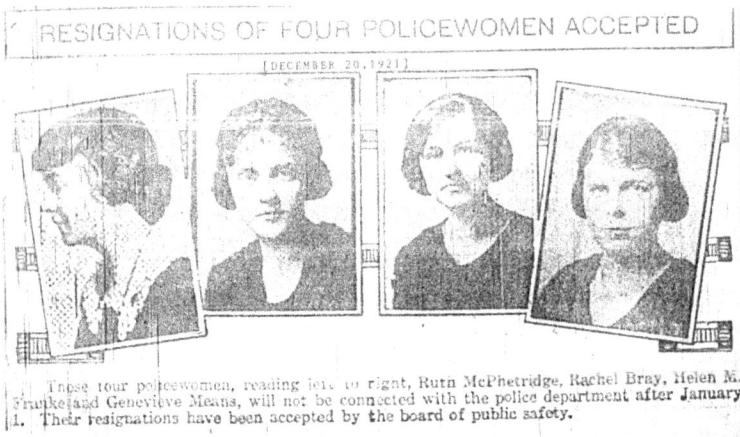

9

On December 18, 1921, Policewomen Genevieve Means, Helen Franke, Ruth McPhetridge and Rachel Bray turned in their resignations. All were under the age of 30 and three were highly educated college graduates.

As they resigned, Genevieve Means and Helen Franke were quoted as saying that since Mayor Lew Shank had taken particular pains to ridicule them whenever he spoke of the women's police department; they believed their retirement might bring about a change in his attitude toward the department. They expressed hope that his

---

[9] IMPD Lichtenberger History Room.

administration would not abolish the women's department as a separate branch of the police department (which he did). The resignations took effect January 1, 1922.

Meanwhile, a committee of women was designing a uniform for the policewomen of Indianapolis. The committee was composed of Irma Byrum, chairman, Mary Moore, Mary Moriarty, Elizabeth Denny and Anna Brunner.

Their unanimous decision was that the official uniform would have plain black buttons on a navy blue uniform. It was to consist of a "strictly tailored suit" of navy blue tricotine and must be hip length.

Each policewoman must wear a black sailor flat and black low-heeled shoes. A special badge would be designed for the policewomen, but they would not be displayed on the uniform. They would be pinned on the inside of the coat and only used if a suspect was placed under arrest. The blouse would be dark blue.

The women of the committee were expected to become new policewomen.

Other changes to the staffing of policewomen included downgrading Laurel C. Thayer, probation officer in the City Court from Sergeant, to policewoman, which she would protest to the Board of Safety.

Pressure had been applied to get three policewomen with the rank of sergeant who were matrons, to retire. Demoted to policewomen on December 28, 1921 were matrons, Sergeants Rena Reisner, Ella Gregoire and Isabelle Phillips. They would be replaced Margaret Hildebrand, Lillian Jaschka and Lourena Fullilove.

On January 2, 1922, major changes occurred among IPD policewomen.

The following policewomen were demoted:

Sgt. Nell Dunkle, to policewoman
Capt. Clara Burnside, to sergeant.
Sgt. Laurel Thayer, to policewoman

The following policewomen turned in their resignations:

Lt. Mary Egan
Mary Mays
Carrie V. Marshall
Margaret B. Hildebrand
Margaret Osborn
Mae Rupert

At the same time, 14 new policewomen were appointed to IPD:

Mary Moore, sergeant, humane dept.
Anna Brunner, sergeant, humane dept.
Elizabeth Denny, sergeant, humane dept.
Lorena Fullilove, turnkey
Edith M. Anthony, detective dept.
Emma Lieber, detective dept.
Cozette E. Osborn, detective dept.
Maude Harris, juvenile court
Irma D. Byram, market house
Mary Moriarty, policewoman
Helen Brewer, policewoman

Sarah D. Murray, policewoman
Mayme E. Shelton, policewoman
Georgina Murphy, policewoman
They joined these policewomen retained
from the previous administration:

Sgt. Clara Burnside, juvenile court
Irene Beyer
Metta Davis
Nell Dunkle
Bertha Duclus
Sadie Osborne
Lillian Jaschka

This made a total of 21 policewomen.

SELECTED TO TEACH POLICEMEN

MRS. GEORGIA MURPHY.

One of them was Georgiana (Robertson) Murphy, 58. Her appointment as Sergeant with the Indianapolis Police Department had been announced December 14th by Mayor-elect Lew Shank.

Shank said that many police officers could not read legibly and that they would need to take an educational test. Georgiana

Murphy had taught school in Indianapolis for 23 years, the last nine, teaching fifth graders at School No. 49, Kappes and Morris Streets.

"I think it is a mighty good idea and I think much can be done by working with the officers," Georgia, as she was known, said. "If I am to teach, I believe the men should be taught the fundamental principles of arithmetic and they should know something of the rules and regulations of weights and measurements and the denominate numbers," she continued.

Georgia's husband Harrison had been struck and killed by a fire truck, December 29, 1918. She had been a Shank supporter in the Tenth Ward during his campaign.

This was one policewoman who didn't work out. On June 14, 1922, the story emerged that she had never reported for duty at headquarters. Her story was that she came to see Chief Rikhoff repeatedly, but he never had time for her.

Police officials didn't catch on that she hadn't reported for duty until June, when Chief Rikhoff issued an order for policewomen to wear uniforms.

Georgia Murphy said she had all the paychecks and would repay the money. She did pay Rikhoff $615.98 on June 17th.

Lew Shank had chosen his tailor, Herman Rikhoff, as his new Chief of Police. He had no law enforcement experience. Shank said, "I know my man is going to be a good chief because he had been my tailor for twenty years. He knows how to make good clothes; he ought to be a good Chief."

Rikhoff had made a trip in December, 1921 to St. Louis and Chicago, among other cities. He said upon his return that police officials there did not look favorably upon policewomen.

In these departments, policewomen were generally scattered through different branches, principally the detective department. He didn't find any department that had a separate division of policewomen as did Indianapolis.

Rikhoff found women over 30 were in other city's detective divisions and he moved mature policewomen in Indianapolis to its detective division.

Chief Rikhoff transferred four policewomen into the Detective Bureau, chosen by Inspector John Mullin. They were Irene Beyer, Cozette Osborn, Bertha Duclus and Nell Dunkle. Joining them a short while later were Sarah D. Murray and Mae Rupert.

As described by *The Indianapolis News* on January 26, 1922, "the first case in the history of the Indianapolis Police Department in which two women detectives were sent to another city to bring back a male prisoner was recorded."

They were referring to Sadie Osborne and Sarah Murray, detectives, driving to Richmond, Indiana on January 25th to arrest Roy Beard, who was charged with contributing to the delinquency of a 17-year old runaway.

The detectives found the girl in a home on North Capitol Avenue and learned from her That Beard met her on the streets of Bedford, Indiana a few days earlier and got her to go with him to Seymour and Indianapolis. She told them Beard went to Richmond.

Beard was arrested at a Richmond hotel, after their investigation had located the girl, who was reported missing. Local police were surprised when the policewomen drove up, as they were expecting male officers.

On the drive back, Sadie Osborne drove, while Sarah Murray guarded the prisoner, shackled to the "robe rod" of the car.

Also on January 26, 1922, Detectives Irene Beyer and Cozette Osborn, along with other detectives, arrested Roy Blocher of Springfield, Ohio and Mrs. Josephine Kinman, of Cincinnati, in a rooming house at 110 East Vermont Street.

They were responding to a complaint of the Kinman woman's husband who said she deserted him and their four small children days ago.

The police department assigned some policewomen to direct traffic for the first time, at various schools, to protect the children. The assignments for their first day on March 16, 1922 were as follows:

Rena Reisner & Mary Moore – St. Joan of Arc school, 42nd and Park.

Emily Holsapple – School No. 54, Dearborn and 10th Streets.

Anna Buck, School No. 49, Morris and Kappes Streets.

Hettie Brewer, School No. 40, Walnut Street and Senate Avenue.

Mamie Shelton, School No. 24, Blake and North Streets.

Emily Holsapple at work, March 21, 1922

At a roll call for the department on April 3, 1922, Mayor Lou Shank told the officers he expected them to cut crime down.

Turning to a group of women working under Sergeant Clara Burnside, he said, "I see we have representatives of the women's police department here this afternoon. This is the first time I have seen much of that part of the force, but so far I have heard of no

---

[10] IMPD Lichtenberger History Room.

trouble in that department. However, they'll have to learn to shoot the same as you men. We are going to take practice and get instructions from competent army officers at Ft. Harrison and from Dr. Thomas B. Noble."

The Indianapolis Police Department's Chief Herman Rikhoff had already instructed Clara on March 31sts to order every woman on the department to obtain a revolver immediately and he told her to arrange with Dr. Thomas Noble Jr. for the women to be taken in squads to a target range to be instructed by him in the use of the weapons.

The mayor was quoted, "They have complained that we have sent policewomen out to catch purse snatchers when they are unarmed. Well, we will see that they are armed and that they know how to use revolvers. Then they will be instructed to begin shooting the minute they see a purse snatching, without even calling to the man to halt."

11

Indianapolis Police Department Range

The policewomen were given training in firearms. On June 28, 1922, four women detectives were taken to the rifle range on the estate of Dr. Noble on the southwest side of town.

According to John Mullin, their scores were comparable to the male officers. Bertha Duclus and Irene Beyer scored bulls-eyes at 20 yards and all of the women scored close to the bulls-eye, using .32 revolvers. Mullin said he was pleased.

---

[11] IMPD Lichtenberger History Room.

STANDARD STYLE OF DRESS FOR
INDIANAPOLIS POLICEWOMEN

Irma Byrum modeling the new uniform

Now Wear Uniforms

POLICEWOMEN MARY MORIARITY AND IRMA BYRUM.

The lady cops are wearing uniforms and are now carrying revolvers and clubs. The pictures of Policewomen Moriarity and Byrum give an idea of their attractiveness.

[12]

---

[12] IMPD Lichtenberger History Room.

On July 1, 1922, the uniform for the policewomen was unveiled. It was designed in December 1921 by a committee of future policewomen. One significant change from what the committee recommended, regarded the badge. The committee wanted it hidden on the inside flap of the coat. The Board of Safety wanted it on the outside of their suits. This did not apply however to the six undercover shoplifting detectives.

Captain John White

The policewomen wearing the uniform reported that afternoon to Chief Rikhoff and Captain John White for inspection. This uniform in one way or another was used through 1925 or so. Another uniform would be unveiled in 1926.

Captain Edward Schubert

Three policewomen who were working out of the Juvenile Court were transferred on August 25, 1922. They would now work directly in the police department under supervision of Captain Edward Schubert.

Anna Brunner was assigned to the information desk in the corridor of police headquarters. Emily Holsapple and Mary Moore were assigned to patrol districts. Holsapple was assigned to district No. 2, on the near southwest side.

Mary Moore was assigned to district No. 6, on the south side of downtown. At this time, the two African-American policewomen, Mayme Shelton and Anna Brewer were patrolling in the districts where most African-Americans resided.

Mayor Lew Shank declared on October 11, 1922 that no more women would be appointed to the Indianapolis Police Department during his administration. He said it had been found impractical to assign policewomen to beats and this practice would be abolished by Chief Rikhoff that morning.

"The police department is no place for a woman," said the mayor. This was less than two months after Policewoman Mary Moore singlehandedly arrested a fleeing male shoplifter on August 25th.

Policewoman Maude Harris

The police department that day ordered Maude Harris, Mary Moore and Cozette Osborn to be assigned to the City Controller's Office to collect delinquent license fees. All women would be assigned somewhere other than police headquarters, with the exception of two teams of women detectives, the prison matrons and information clerk (Anna Brunner).

In December 1922, Herman Rikhoff was told by Mayor Shank that he'd like to "get rid of about ten of these women police."

In early January, Mayor Shank had assigned three policewomen (Anna Buck, Emily Holsapple and Hettie Brewer) to the City Hospital to guard female prisoners in the detention ward. The policewomen knew that the previous women assigned to this job had also been used as nurses in the contagious ward. They complained to Shank about this.

Rikhoff said if the women had gone to him instead of the mayor to complain, he would have suspended them and filed charges against them with the board of safety.

"These women don't do any work and they are incompetent. Why should they stay on the pay roll when they don't do anything? This was the mayor's chance to get rid of them this morning, but he didn't take it."

Chief Herman Rikhoff sent a letter to the Board of Safety on January 8, 1923, recommending Sergeant Elizabeth Denny be reduced to the rank of patrolman. She was the only policewoman with IPD who held that rank at present. Rikhoff also recommended that the resignation of Policewoman Maude Harris, submitted that day, be accepted.

Rikhoff further recommended that four policewomen (including the three who didn't want to go to the hospital detention ward) be transferred to the City Controller's office to collect license fees. Joseph L. Hogue, the city controller, only wanted one policewoman to collect delinquent license fees and he had obtained her earlier in the day.

On January 11th, Mayor Shank announced that policewomen Emily Holsapple, Anna Buck and Hettie Brewer were assigned to the traffic department to work under Captain Michael Glenn.

Captain Michael Glenn

Captain Glenn sent them out to arrest persons who hadn't changed their automobile licenses.

"They can stay there awhile," grudgingly remarked Chief Rikhoff.

(They were then sent after a few days to the Juvenile Court, "the only work for which they are adapted", he said).

Two of the three (Buck and Holsapple) publicly disputed Rikhoff's statement that policewomen, as a whole, are incompetent and inefficient, on January 11th.

Rikhoff did think that some women were essential to IPD: Rachel Bray, his stenographer; Anna Brunner, information desk; Matrons Lillian Jaschka, Lourena Fullilove and Elizabeth Denny; the women assigned to the Juvenile Court and the Detective Department, and those assigned to the terminal Station.

The situation between Mayor Lew Shank and Chief Herman Rikhoff and the policewomen of Indianapolis broke wide open on January 11, 1923. *The Indianapolis News* published a lengthy article detailing how the city administration had renewed the efforts they'd made since assuming office to get the policewomen to leave the department.

The News' position was that virtually all other cities in 1923 were being used in social services work as a prevention of crime and this was the case in Indianapolis until the Shank administration took office in January 1922.

Since then, Shank and Rikhoff had moved the policewomen from one assignment to another, nearly always disagreeable to the women. The policewomen had been reduced in rank, required to wear uniforms and badges and carry revolvers. They had also been assigned to patrolling beats. Many policewomen, who had been regarded as efficient before 1922, had resigned.

On January 13, 1923, a possible solution to the problem of where to put Buck, Holsapple and Brewer came with the establishment of a municipal division of housing and sanitation, working in conjunction with the board of public health.

Mayor Shank announced that the division would have five policewomen in it and would be responsible for cleaning up housing and unsanitary conditions. The policewomen would be Anna Buck, Emily

Holsapple, Mary Moore, Hettie Brewer and Irene Beyer, who would be in charge.

Chief Rikhoff took exception to the Mayor moving the policewomen because he had moved them on paper to the Juvenile Branch and wanted them to stay there.

Trouble for the policewomen started on January 14th. Chief Herman Rikhoff had seen reports that Emily Holsapple and Anna Buck had "viciously" attacked the city administration, Mayor Shank and himself.

He said Holsapple had criticized him and threatened to "expose" him, among other threats.

Rikhoff ordered police to the home of Policewoman Anna Buck, 834 West 31st Street, to get her badge. She declined to surrender it and she called Chief Rikhoff on January 15th. Rikhoff said her attitude was not defiant.

Emily Holsapple personnel sheet.

On Sunday, January 14th, Sergeants John Corrigan and Harry Nageleisen took an official request from Chief Rikhoff for Emily Holsapple to give up her badge. She laughed and said an army of male police

L-R: Sergeants John Corrigan and Harry Nagleisen, who came for Holsapple's badge.

Sergeants might get her badge, "But two!

Never!" She was suspended that day. She did agree to see the chief the next day.

Chief Herman Rikhoff

Monday, she entered Rikhoff's office ready to fight. According to the chief, "She smiled and sneered when I spoke to her, refusing to obey my command to turn in her badge and threatened to 'tell a whole lot of things' if I took the matter up with the Board of Safety."

Regarding Anna Buck, although he had heard reports of her making wild statements about him, when they sat down in person, she denied she had criticized the chief or refused to obey his orders. He said her attitude was respectful.

Emily Holsapple - 1922

In the end, Anna Buck was allowed to keep her job while Emily Holsapple was charged with insubordination and inefficiency on January 16th.

At an all-day hearing before the Board of Public Safety on January 30, 1923, Policewoman Emily Holsapple faced charges of insubordination. During the hearing, around 60 witnesses testified in front of an audience of 200 people. Her attorney Ira Holmes contended that the heads of the police department attempted to get rid of the department of women by assigning them to bad beats and other unpleasant duties.

Chief of Police Herman Rikhoff countered that Officer Holsapple was guilty of insubordination, inefficiency and specifically, failure to turn in her badge, as ordered.

Judge Frank J. Lahr of Juvenile court and Miss Clara Burnside, adult probation officer of the court, testified that in their opinion Mrs. Holsapple was not an efficient policewoman.

Several witnesses of the sixty-two subpoenaed by Mrs. Holsapple, testified concerning incidents in which the policewoman appeared efficient. About fifty women spectators were members of civic clubs that have protested against Mrs.

Holsapple's removal from the police
department.

On February 7, 1923, the Board of Safety
found Holsapple guilty and dismissed her
from the department.

Society Women Join IPD

Detective Emma (Rappaport) Lieber

In 1921, while a private citizen, an
Indianapolis socialite, Mrs. Emma Lieber
decided to meet with mayor-elect Samuel
"Lew" Shank with concerns she had about
his plans for female policewomen. This is
an article she wrote about her experience,
which led her to join IPD.

"When at our recent change of city administration the mayor-elect had decided that policewomen were an unnecessary expense upon the taxpayer and calmly and coolly arranged to disband our women's police department, which under the splendid leadership of Miss Clara Burnside had gained a national reputation.

I felt very much perturbed. Having been a close observer of the work of our police women and having learned that their method of preventive work had done much to eliminate delinquency, especially among young girls; I naturally became very much disturbed over the conclusion at which our mayor-elect had arrived.

I took it upon myself to call upon Mr. Shank and explain to him in a dispassionate manner the work that had been done by our women's police department. Advisedly I say "In a dispassionate manner." as I had no selfish motive in mind. I was neither looking for office nor for a Job. My work as a social worker had always been volunteer service.

I admit that Mr. Shank was not very much impressed with my visit, nor, for that matter, with the argument that I used in urging him to reconsider his plan of destroying an agency that I claimed had been of such vital benefit to the citizens of our fair city. However, after a number of talks with the mayor-elect I had made such headway that he asked me to consider an appointment.

Perhaps for this reason he appointed me and another clubwoman as observers or investigators for the police department, saying that If I could after two or three months' service, prove to him that women on the police force were an asset to the city, he would be willing to reorganize this department.

MRS. OTTO ANTHONY.

Detective Edith May (McFarland) Anthony

My partner (Edith M. Anthony) and I were formally appointed January 1, 1922, to serve on the Indianapolis police force until we could work out a plan for women police that seemed feasible and desirable to the mayor and the board of safety. We were to give seven hours service a day, to divide our time as we saw fit.

We were given police power, but were asked not to make arrests. We were told to divide our time between the jail and courthouse, visiting the different courts and especially observing methods that were used in handling prisoners. We were to keep our eyes open but our mouths closed and report directly to the mayor.

The first thing I did was to acquaint myself with the details of the system of our police department. I asked the chief of police to assign me one officer who could show me through the police station and could explain the method of work of the officers.

Indianapolis has about 430 patrolmen on the force at the present time. These patrol the 58 districts. There are 68 detectives, six of whom are women. Besides this, Indianapolis has 21 women in different departments in the police force.

At the beginning of this article I stated that I called upon Mayor Shank for the purpose of inducing him to retain women on the Indianapolis police force, explaining to him the protective and preventive work they have done. I was able after a few months' investigation to bring to his attention many cases which bad been handled by policewomen and which had not at any time been brought into court.

These cases were adjusted in the women's police department. In conclusion I am most happy to say that Mayor Shank accepted the report and the recommendations, which were submitted to him March 1, 1922. Note: Officers Emma (Rappaport) Lieber and Edith (McFarland) Anthony did spend 3 months with the Indianapolis Police Department as originally agreed to with Mayor Shank.

Chief Herman Rikhoff announced on March 26, 1924 that he was calling for a conference in his office March 29th with dance hall matrons, policewomen and social service workers, among others. The subject would be on how to prevent the evils existing in public dance halls.

"The problem is a big one – one which one person should not try to solve alone," Chief Rikhoff said. This meeting was the result of a report filed March 24th by Policewoman Anna Brunner to the chief, calling attention to conditions in local dance halls. She recommended either more dance matrons be appointed, or the existing ones paying closer attention to the problem.

In October of 1925, three bandits escaped from a robbery scene, despite two IPD officers firing multiple times at them. In response, Chief Rikhoff ordered every man- and woman on the department to undergo firearms training.

Women Officers Practice for Deadly Bandit War

Leona Foppiano and Rachael Bray.

"Shoot to kill!"

This is the motto of Policewomen Leona Foppiano and Rachael Bray. They are partaking in target practice at orders of Mayor Shank. Mayor Shank ordered practice for all police. A range has been established in the basement of the police station. Capt. Roy Pope and Capt. Barrett Ball are in charge.

Police to hold their jobs must make a score of 40 out of a possible 50 in ten shots.

13

Two policewomen aided a squad of police in a raid of the rooming house at 415 North Illinois Street on December 12, 1925.

The raid was led by Lieutenant Orville "Jiggers" Hudson, head of the "booze squad" during prohibition. In the past, attempted

Lieutenant Orville Hudson

raids here had failed because a doorman warned the residents, who emptied the liquor before police could get in. This time, Hudson sent Detectives Cozette Osborn and

Josephine Fairhead, to the door, armed with a search warrant.

The policewomen were admitted, and before the doorman could shut the door, Hudson jumped inside and while the women kept talking loudly, he grabbed Isaac Sherman, lookout at the door. Jiggers put his hand over Sherman's mouth to prevent a warning cry and the policemen followed the policewomen up the stairs.

There they found three men and two women and arrested them. They confiscated a gallon of whiskey.

Only a month later, on January 4, 1926, Mayor John L. Duvall suspended 115 police officers saying there was no room in the budget for their salaries. Only one, Policewoman Josephine Fairhead refused to turn in her badge, saying the Board of Safety had no right to suspend her without charges. Chief of Police Johnson said she would be brought up on charges. She resigned before the trial of 125 city employees.

Another policewoman who lost her job in this action was Alma E. Baker. Like Fairhead, she had only been on the job a month. A stenographer in Mayor Lew Shank's office, she was appointed a policewoman November 27, 1925.

At the police roll call, Friday, January 8, 1926, it was announced that most of the 24 policewomen had new assignments. These changes included assignments to the bus terminal, Union Station, the city market and the creation of a missing person's bureau.

Leona Foppiano

Policewoman Leona Foppiano would head the missing person's bureau. Chief Claude F. Johnson, after conferring with Sergeant Rachel Bray Schwier the previous day, who was in charge of all policewomen, felt this would give the policewomen more mobility.

That same day it was announced that Sergeant Schwier would be responsible for approving daily dance permits.

Women Named on Police Force

Miss Alma Baker

Mrs. Josephine Fairhead

Two women were on the list of forty-eight named to the police force by Mayor Shank and the board of safety. Miss Alma Baker is now a stenographer in Mayor Shank's office and Mrs. Josephine Fairhead is telephone operator at city hall.

POLICE WOMAN — Miss Alma E. Baker, stenographer in the mayor's office, who will become a member of the city force.

14

---

14 IMPD Lichtenberger History Room, December 1, 1925.

She was suspended February 9, 1926 when she didn't quit and was dismissed February 11th when she didn't show up for the trial (along with Josephine Fairhead and Policewoman Frieda Sonderman. A month later Alma Baker was employed as a stenographer for the Marion County Assessor.

Emma Christy was born in Salem,
Washington County, Indiana on February
10, 1865 to William W. Christy and Hester
Shrewsberry.

Emma's grandfather was Drayton Christy,
born a free man of color in North Carolina.
He had three sons among his large family
who moved to Indianapolis, Indiana:
William W. (1843-1934), Levi E. (1850-1923)
and Leroy D.S. Christy (1856-1899).

Southern Indiana was populated largely
with Whites transplanted from southern
states such as Virginia and North Carolina
and during the Civil War; many of these
men took a pro-Confederate stance. They
were known as "Copper heads".

The attitudes of these men toward African-Americans in their community became hardened after Lincoln signed the Emancipation Proclamation in 1863. They didn't feel that African-American people should be made equal to Whites.

The people of Indiana were astounded when Confederate General John Hunt Morgan led his cavalry across the Ohio River from Kentucky into Indiana on July 8, 1863. The countryside went into a panic and troops were mobilized in Indianapolis. On July 10th, Morgan's Raiders arrived in Salem and the few local men who thought they could stand them off fled when they saw them arriving at the court house.

The Confederates ransomed the town, threatening to burn the local mills unless each miller paid them $1,000. They then proceeded to burn the railroad depot, two railroad bridges and destroy other property on their way east. There were threats made during this raid to send any African-American people they encountered back south into slavery.

MORGAN'S RAID INTO INDIANA—THE CONFEDERATE GUERILLAS DESTROYING AND PILLAGING THE DEPOT AND STORES AT SALEM, INDIANA, JULY 10.—FROM A SKETCH BY C. E. HASKINS.

Morgan's Raiders Pillage Salem, Indiana, July 10, 1863

From 1863 onward, a systematic pattern of intimidation, violence and murder occurred in the Salem area by White people against the African-American inhabitants. This is keyed into the selling of property by the Christy family and their migration out of the area,

In December 1864, John Williams, one of the African-American residents who had lived in the community the longest and was undoubtedly well known by the Christy family, was shot to death outside his home. Nothing about his death was printed in the local papers and no action was taken to find his killer or killers. Years later it was written that this was a racially motivated slaying by a longtime resident.

An account from the Indianapolis News, on June 11, 1892, states that William W. Christy came to Indianapolis in 1863.

Hester M. Shrewsberry was born in 1844, Monticello, Wayne County, Kentucky to Richard Shrewsberry. She and her parents were slaves. In 1849, their owners moved to Washington County, Indiana which was a free state. Their owners freed their slaves and encouraged them to make new homes for themselves.

The *Indianapolis Recorder* wrote on June 11, 1932. "Mrs. Emma Baker, an old citizen of Indianapolis, was born in Salem, Indiana and was brought to this city when a mere babe, one month old."

The first employment William Christy found in Indianapolis was that of a coachman. The Indianapolis City Directory of 1865 shows him working as a waiter at the Bates House, a famous hotel on Washington Street. They were among the first African-American land owners in Indianapolis.

One month after Emma Christy arrived in Indianapolis, the State Capitol was draped in black when the body of Abraham Lincoln lay in state. [15]

The family settled by 1867 at 318 West North Street, on the near west side of town.

[15] Old Indiana State Capitol Draped in Mourning for Abraham Lincoln, April 1865. University of Indianapolis Digital Mayoral Archives. http://uindy.historyit.com/item/recordview.php?itemid=834458&record=199103&ftype=jpg (accessed 3/4/2017). - See more at: http://uindy.historyit.com/item/recordview.php?itemid=834458&record=199103&ftype=jpg#sthash.0TQDQmK0.dpuf

He then worked at an express office. William changed jobs and residences several times over the next few years. William opened up a laundry business by 1875 at 166 Blake Street. This business would prosper in the coming years.

In 1876, the City of Indianapolis decided to try an experiment and appoint African-American men to the Fire Department and Police Department. William W. Christy put in an application. Five men were appointed to each department but William's name was not among them. He was probably passed over because the department had enough men who were Republicans on the department, which was extremely politicized then.

By 1876, Emma Christy was enrolled in the public schools of Indianapolis. Education was heavily emphasized in her family. Her father's brother, Levi Christy in 1876 was principal of School No. 19, on the west side of South Pennsylvania Street in Indianapolis.

William W. Christy, still interested in working in law enforcement, was nominated by the Democratic Party for the office of City Marshal of Indianapolis on April 12, 1879. This made national news due to the fact Christy was African-American. Unfortunately, he lost in the general election May 6th, 8,769 to 4,611 votes.

Levi Christy

In 1880, while Emma's Uncle Levi taught school during the day, he took special night courses of study under tutors from Yale

University.   He resigned from IPS in 1885 to become editor and co-owner with his brother Leroy of the *Indianapolis World*, the 2nd African-American newspaper in Indianapolis.   They operated the paper out of 359 Blake Street, location of their brother William Christy's laundry business.

The first time Emma is mentioned in a newspaper was on December 17, 1881 in the Indianapolis News. She, sister Cora and several other young ladies were assisting the ladies of the Bethel A.M.E. Church on Vermont Street Church in holding an open house at the church, January 2, 1882. The paper urged the "young gents" in the community to call on them.   That night, Emma and Cora worked as waitresses, serving ice cream, coffee and cakes to the guests.

Emma was a lifelong member of the Bethel A.M.E. Church (1950).

Emma Christy graduated from Booker T. Washington Public School No. 17, 1102 North West Street and then went onto Shortridge High School, where she graduated about 1884.

Shortridge High School - 1894[16]

She then began helping her father in the laundry business. She met a man named David M. Baker, born January 22, 1867 in Redwood, Illinois to John and Laura (Booth) Baker of Illinois. On July 9, 1889 in Indianapolis, they were married. Emma then went into business for herself.

---

[16] The High School Annual – June 1894, courtesy Digital Indy.

A very young Emma Christy

The Christy family was doing pretty well by 1892. Emma's father was estimated to be worth $12,000, most of which was in real estate. Emma remained in business for herself through 1899. She and David Baker had one son, John William D. Baker, born January 22, 1892. "Will" Baker died at age 7, July 7, 1899. He was buried in Crown Hill Cemetery.

In 1900, David Baker was a barber and he and Emma lived at 639 Blake Street. Her parents resided next door at 643 Blake Street. Her sister Cora Christy was employed as a school teacher at School No. 24. She made a career of teaching school. In 1903, she married Lucas B. Willis, who became a successful funeral director in Indianapolis.

Emma kept herself busy with club activity, for example hosting the Topaz Cluster Club in March of 1900. She continued with this club through 1929.

At some time between 1900 and 1910, Emma Baker began running her father's laundry business on Blake Street.

LAUNDRY.

LAUNDRY—CHRISTY LAUNDRY; all work done by hand. New phone 2773.

1909 ad for the William Christy laundry.

Husband David was still barbering in 1910. Cora Willis was one of the founding members of the Indianapolis Chapter of the N.A.A.C.P., serving as its treasurer on May 24, 1913, when its constitution was approved.

Hester Christy, mother of Emma, became ill and died shortly afterward, February 3, 1915 at her home on Blake Street. Emma Baker was involved in club activity. On January 14, 1916, she entertained the Art Club at her Blake Street home. She was still hosting the Art Club in 1918.

When the Board of Public Safety was looking at applications for policewomen in 1918, they saw that Emma Baker was well known in the African-American community and therefore, knew of the conditions there. She was one of two black women appointed. William Christy must have been proud to see his daughter accomplish something he had tried to do in 1876.

Emma Baker's personnel file shows she was assigned badge number 1 on June 15, 1918. At the end of her probation period she was issued badge number 66.

On July 2, 1918, Captain Clara Burnside announced the new assignments for the policewomen. Emma and Mary's beat would run from 1:30 p.m. to 11:30 p.m.

There were two distinct neighborhoods populated by African-Americans in 20th century Indianapolis. The oldest was known as "Pat Ward's Bottoms" and was located on the northwest side of town, along the canal, on W. 11th Street. It was established during and after the Civil War. It was part of the 34th District. This included Indiana Avenue.

The second was farther north of that area, along what is now known as Dr. Martin Luther King Jr. Street. This area seems to correspond with what 40-year IPD veteran "Jack" Hadley described as "old District 35", an area between 9th and 16th Streets and West Street and Capitol Avenue. This was his first assignment in 1920.

Indiana Avenue – One of the main beats for
Officers Baker and Mays

The first statistical report on the work that Emma Baker and Mary Mays were doing came out on November 7, 1918, covering the month of October. Here's the rundown:

45 cases of girls, 14 women, 26 boys & men on charges of neglect and drunkenness.

The Indianapolis Star reported on December 21, 1918 that Mary Mays and Emma Baker, "policewomen for the colored district", had so far in December found two "blind tigers" (speak-easy) and reported

them to Captain Burnside. They had
investigated complaints of 27 girls, ten
women and 24 boys.

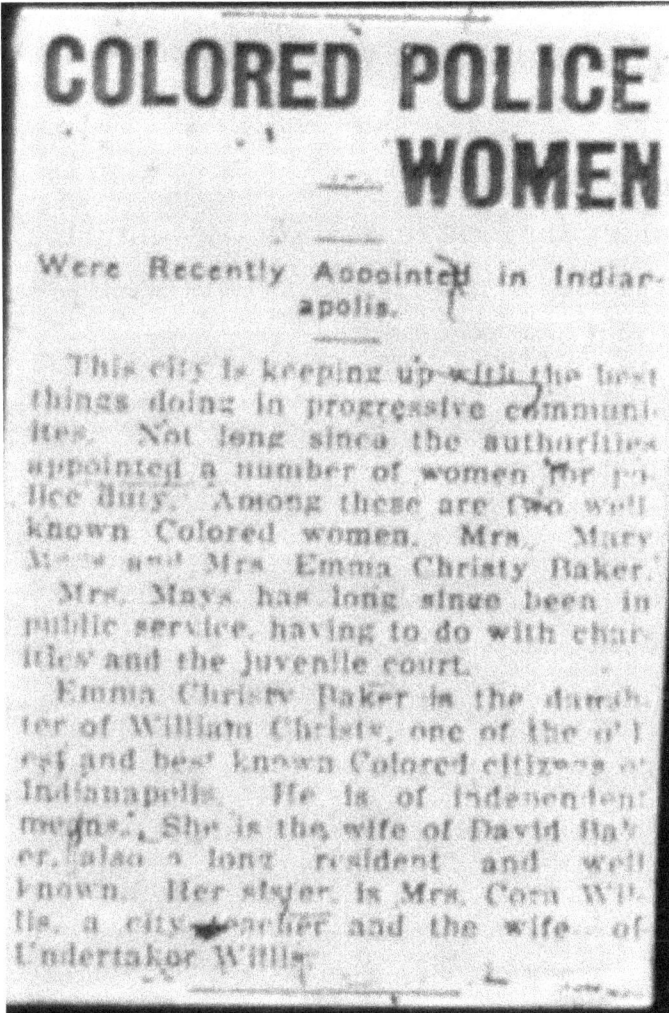

COLORED POLICE WOMEN

Were Recently Appointed in Indianapolis.

This city is keeping up with the best
things doing in progressive communities. Not long since the authorities
appointed a number of women for police duty. Among these are two well
known Colored women, Mrs. Mary
Mays and Mrs. Emma Christy Baker.

Mrs. Mays has long since been in
public service, having to do with charities and the juvenile court.

Emma Christy Baker is the daughter of William Christy, one of the oldest and best known Colored citizens of
Indianapolis. He is of independent
means. She is the wife of David Baker, also a long resident and well
known. Her sister is Mrs. Cora Willis, a city teacher and the wife of
Undertaker Willis.

Emma worked out of police headquarters
until 1922. At that point she was

transferred to the Juvenile Court in the Probation Department. She worked out of the Marion County Courthouse after that. On March 31, 1922, it was announced that all IPD policewomen would be allowed to carry guns.

They had been arresting men as well as women, for four years. They would have to purchase their own weapon but would be trained on their use.

Mrs. Max Young	Asst. Probation Officer
Mrs. Mary Lane	Asst. Probation Officer
Mrs. Emma Lott	Asst. Probation Officer
Miss Lucetta T. Ohr	Asst. Probation Officer
Mrs. Mette Davis	Asst. Probation Officer
Mrs. Margaret Hildebrandt	Asst. Probation Officer
Mrs. Emma Baker	Asst. Probation Officer
Mrs. Genevieve Edwards	Asst. Probation Officer

Above Emma Baker – Probation Officer, 1922.

In March 1924, Emma Baker assisted Policewoman Hettie Brewer (African-American), on Saturday nights, working as a Dance Matron at the dance halls frequented by African-Americans.

At this time, one of the policewomen assigned as Dance Matron had reported the matrons were very understaffed to patrol all of the dance halls in town. "Cheek to cheek dancing" and couples moving dancing in a small area without moving around were rampant. Hettie and Emma were both paid a salary of $1,733.50 a year in 1924.

Officer Emma Baker worked out of the Marion County Court House after 1922.[17] – 1925 photograph.

[17] Second Marion County Courthouse, 1925. University of Indianapolis Digital Mayoral Archives.
http://uindy.historyit.com/item/recordview.php?itemid=846705&record=213614&ftype=jpg (accessed 3/4/2017). - See more at:
http://uindy.historyit.com/item/recordview.php?itemid=846705&record=213614&ftype=jpg#sthash.QOyiQwzA.dpuf

About 1924, left to right: Det. Sgt. George Sneed, Det. Sgt. Edward Trabue and Policewoman Emma Baker.

In July 1928 at 8 a.m., David M. Baker had some sort of an accident, breaking his right forearm. Perhaps he was comatose, unable to explain how the accident occurred. He died in City Hospital August 19, 1928 after 25 days of a heart attack. He was buried in Crown Hill Cemetery.

In May, 1929, Emma hosted a meeting of the Social Workers Fellowship at her home on Blake Street. Speaking to the group was Mr. Foster of the Indianapolis Foundation Society.

Emma joined the Old Settlers Civic and Social Club in 1929, which would be an interest of hers for the rest of her life. Lucas B. Willis, brother-in-law of Emma Baker, passed away on March 22, 1930. His funeral parlor was located at 510 North West Street, residence at 512 North West Street.

On March 28, 1930, the Ohio Valley regional conference of the Child Welfare League of America was held at the Claypool Hotel. Mrs. Emma Baker of Juvenile Court attended these sessions on March 28-29th.

Emma Baker

In July of 1931, there were four African-Americans on the Juvenile Court staff, including Emma, the only policewoman among them. They had charge of any African-American children coming through the court system.

Emma Baker was profiled in the Indianapolis Recorder, June 11, 1932. The paper credited her with saving numerous juveniles from a life of crime through her

befriending of them and her wise counsel.
Also, her work made the parents of these
youth redouble their efforts in good
parenting. Emma was described as being
well liked by everyone and standing out as a
remarkable woman of her race.

On October 17, 1932, the City-Council
passed an ordinance that created more
grades among the rank of Patrolman with
the Indianapolis Police Department. The
fifteen then serving policewomen were
moved into these new, lower ranks. Emma
Baker was downgraded from Second Grade
Patrolman to Fifth Grade Patrolman with a
cut in salary to $1,000 annually.

By 1936, Emma Baker moved into her sister
Cora's home at 512 North West Street. The
siblings, who had been as close as sisters
could be all their lives, spent their
remaining years here.

In February of 1937, Emma estimated that
she had handled over 3,000 juvenile cases
since 1923, many of them resulting in
convictions. Her feeling was that many of

these troubled children were created from a lack of communication between their parents. She went to the trouble of trying to find relief or jobs for some of the parents she dealt with. She chased or tracked down many other renegade parents across town to bring them together for the good of the child.

In her relentless pursuit of neglectful parents, Emma related one story of an epic chase. "I chased her for three days without stopping. I was trying to get this interview and we had a foot chase all through the court house from court room to waiting room but I wouldn't give up. I finally caught her in her private office. I stopped, barring the door-way. There was only one means of escape – give me the interview. She was displeased over me following her around. I was displeased over her having made me follow her around, too. But I won. We parted friends."

Emma Baker commented to a reporter in 1937 that she only had one problem with her job. She didn't have a car. Problem was she couldn't drive.

As part of her job, Officer Emma Baker occasionally gave public talks about a subject she knew very well by now, that of juvenile delinquency. One such occasion came on March 16, 1938. She addressed members of School No. 56 that night. Her subject was "What to Do with Delinquent Boys and Girls."

The following week, on March 22nd, the Indianapolis Police Department made an innovation in the fight against juvenile delinquency. They opened up a new Police Department crime prevention bureau for juvenile law violators that morning.

It was headed by Sergeant Charles E. Weddle and staffed by Policewomen Nell Dunkle, Bertha L. Duclus and Emma Baker. From now on, juvenile offenders would be brought directly to the Juvenile Bureau on the 2nd floor of police headquarters and not go to court. Every effort was made there to question the children and determine what the underlying causes of their misbehavior was, before taking them to court.

Emma Baker turned in her retirement papers, which the Board of Safety approved, August 5, 1939. She was 74 years old but said she was 70.

Emma Baker got involved in Indianapolis politics in October 1947. She was made a member of a 70-person Special Committee of African-American citizens with the goal of getting Republican candidate William H. Wemmer elected Mayor.

Her name was one of 35 prominent citizens who endorsed Wemmer, November 1, 1947. Wemmer lost by 8,361 votes on November 4th. The former Willis B. Lucas funeral home was the location of the Indianapolis Chapter of the N.A.A.C.P. from October 1948-January 1952.

Late in life, Emma Baker was still very active with her clubs. The May 26, 1951 meeting of the meeting of the Loyal Legion Club of Bethel AME Church was attended by members Cora Willis, Mrs. Emma Baker and Alberta Tucker (their cousin). On March 19, 1954, the Old Settlers Social and Civic Club met to appoint committee chairmen. Emma was appointed chairman of housing. She was then 89 years old. Throughout her life, Emma only had one hobby – bridge.

Emma Baker was sick and homebound for the last year of her life. Her arteries were becoming blocked. On September 23, 1955, she died in her home, aged 90. Her place in history was properly noted in all of the local newspapers.

She was the first African-American woman and the first woman, period, to serve as a Policewoman in the City of Indianapolis (if not the State of Indiana). However, her only living relative at this time was her sister Cora, now aged 89, herself. A tombstone was never purchased for Emma, her husband David or their son John.

From 1955-2002, Emma's memory was kept barely alive, more-so after the institution of

African-American History Month, where she became an African-American "first". Her early partner, Mary E. Mays, had been almost completely forgotten, due to the fact she died in 1928 in Los Angeles. Emma had no children, or even nieces or nephews, to carry on her memory. Her sister Cora, who was childless, died in 1958. Their only living cousin, Alberta (Christy) Turner, also died childless.

One known distant relative, Meta L. Christy (1895-1968), achieved her own measure of fame. Born in Kokomo, Indiana to a cousin of Emma's grandfather, Meta graduated in 1921 from the Philadelphia College of Osteopathic Medicine. She was their first minority student. She is recognized as the *world's* first African-American osteopath. It is not known if she knew of her pioneering cousin in Indianapolis.

In 2003, the author decided to research the life of Emma (Christy) Baker and published an article in the Indianapolis Police Department newsletter about her and the fact she had no tombstone. This story touched Officer Marilyn Gurnell of IPD, who was born the same year Emma died. Assigned to the Police Athletic League, she taught students in her G.R.E.A.T. (Gang Resistance and Training) class.

The goal is to keep them from joining gangs. She is following in Emma Baker's footsteps in a way. The class needed a project to graduate. Officer Gurnell chose the task of raising the estimated $3,000 to purchase a proper headstone for Emma Baker, her husband David and their son Will.

This was a daunting task. The project was taken up by 400 IPS schoolchildren (appropriate, considering the involvement of Cora Willis her whole life teaching public school here). They went door to door, raising many dollars. The Fraternal Order of Police Lodge #86 in Indianapolis and local businesses also donated to the cause. This project reached its fruition on September 23, 2003, the anniversary of Emma Baker's death.

On that day, the leaders of the Indianapolis Police Department (Chief of Police Jerry Barker and Assistant Chief Deborah Saunders, highest ranking African-American woman in department history), the Marion County Sheriff, Frank Anderson, the first African-American Sheriff in Marion County history, and the Indiana State Police (Superintendent Melvin Carroway, first African-American head of that agency), met for the dedication ceremony. Today, Emma (Christy) Baker is on the tour of historic African-Americans in the Crown Hill Cemetery.

Dedication ceremony

Marilyn Gurnell (top) after the dedication ceremony, with her husband Edward Gurnell.

Marilyn Gurnell decorating Emma's unmarked grave.

Indiana Historical Society Display

Emma Christy Baker

INDIANAPOLIS
JUN
7
2016
46298

FIRST DAY OF ISSUE

Emma Christy Baker (February 10, 1865 – September 23, 1955) was well known in Indianapolis for her laundry business and presence around town. During World War I, however, she was recruited to become one of the city's first Black police officers and one of 13 women in the Indianapolis Police Department's all-female unit. A few years later, her all-woman police unit had become the largest in the world with 23 officers. By the end of the 1930s, the all-woman police unit had been disbanded. It wasn't until 1968 that women would again be assigned to street-duty in Indianapolis. Officer Emma Baker retired March 15, 1939, at age 74. She remained involved in local politics and charitable efforts.

First edition "cachet" issued to honor Emma Christy Baker, 2016.

New Administration Purges Women

Over the years, the city administration had changed its outlook on the usefulness of policewomen. World War I had ended and the manpower shortage was over.

Mayor Jewett and Chief George Coffin had been replaced by men who did not look on policewomen the same way, Mayor Lew Shank and Chief Herman Rikhoff.

The salaries and assignments of the Indianapolis policewomen in February 1924 were as follows:

Mary C. Moore, secretary, accident prevention - $2,000.00
Emma Baker, investigator, $1,733.50
Irene Beyer, file clerk, accident prevention, $1,733.50
Rachel Bray, stenographer to chief, $1,733.50
Anna Brunner, information clerk, $1,733.50
Anna Buck, patrol woman, $1,733.50
Irma Byrum, patrol woman, $1,733.50

Mary Cantlon, patrol woman, $1,733.50
Metta Davis, patrol woman, $1,733.50
Elizabeth Denny, prison matron, $1,733.50
Nell Dunkle, patrol woman, $1,733.50
Bertha Duclus, patrol woman, $1,733.50
Lourena Fullilove, prison matron, $1,733.50
Margaret Hildebrand, patrol woman,
$1,733.50
Lillian Jaschka, prison matron, $1,733.50
Mary Moriarty, patrol woman, $1,733.50
Cozette Osborn, patrol woman, $1,733.50
Sadie Osborne, file clerk, detective
department, $1,733.50
Sara Rogers, patrol woman, $1,733.50

Male patrolmen also made $1,733.50 so
there was parity here.

When the 32nd annual convention of the
International Association of Chiefs of Police
was held in Indianapolis in July 1925, Chief
Herman Rikhoff appointed the following
policewomen to the women's reception
committee who would be in charge of the
entertainment of the visiting officials: Mary
Moriarty, Irma Byrum, Rachel Bray and
Leona Foppiano.

John L. Duvall

In January 1926, the new Mayor of
Indianapolis was John L. Duvall.   On
March 5, 1926, a presentation of service
badges for longevity with the police
department was made at the women's roll
call. Chief of Police Claude F. Johnson and
Sergeant Rachel Bray Schwier made the
presentations. The women who received the
service badges were:

Emma Baker - 7 years, 8 months.
Irene Beyer - 7 years, 8 months.
Anna Buck - 7 years, 8 months.
Bertha Duclus – 7 years, 8 months.
Lillian Jaschka – 7 years, 8 months.
Sadie Osborne – 7 years, 8 months.
Mary Cantlon – 6 years.
Margaret Hildebrand – 6 years.
Metta Davis – 5 years.
Nell Dunkle – 5 years.

The Board of Public Safety on April 27, 1926, decreed that IPD policewomen would have new uniforms. These uniforms would be dark blue tailored suits with a sailor hat of felt or straw, as the season demands.

The uniform would include a .38 caliber revolver with a one-inch barrel. This was something Chief Claude F. Johnson wanted done. Up to now, eight policewomen currently walking beats were carrying a variety of weapons, if they even carried one. Chief Johnson was recommending that all policemen carry .38 special revolvers. Motorcycle officers were then carrying .45's.

UNIFORMS RECENTLY DONNED BY POLICEWOMEN

"Black silk stockings, a part of the new uniforms donned by Indianapolis policewomen Monday for the first time, are the only part of the uniform the women don't like, according to Miss Leona Foppiano, of the missing person's department at police headquarters.

The twenty-three policewomen made a striking appearance in the blue serge suits, white waists, blue ties, black silk stockings and black straw hats. The suits are trimmed in black braid.
'I think they're just darling, don't you?' Miss Rachael Bray, sergeant of policewomen,

said of the uniforms. The order for the new uniforms applies to matrons as well as policewomen and was issued by Claude F. Johnson, chief of police.

Chief Johnson is very well pleased with the appearance of the policewomen. His orders also provide that the women carry a .38 special revolver strapped in a holster."

The Indianapolis News – June 14, 1926

The Indianapolis city budget was strained in 1926. There was a proposal made on July 14, 1926 to add about 120 employees to the pay roll and add about one half million dollars to current expenditures.

Regarding the police department, estimates provided for the addition of 71 men and the discharge of 10 policewomen. This would increase the police payroll by $144,000.

The plan was for policewomen assigned to office work, but drawing full pay as officers would be replaced by clerks and stenographers at lower salaries. There were then 22 policewomen.   On November 30, 1926, Chief Johnson was now talking about eliminating 17 policewomen.

The board of directors of the Indianapolis League of Women Voters sent letters on December 3, 1926 to Mayor John L. Duvall and Chief Claude F. Johnson, protesting the proposed reduction of policewomen from 21 to 5. The letters requested the number be no less than 16 policewomen.

Judge Frank J. Lahy of the Juvenile Court, which had four policewomen on his staff, also registered a protest. He pointed out that the policewomen perform the job better than any man.

On the afternoon of Tuesday, December 28, 1926, 15 policewomen were ordered dropped from the police force by the Board of Safety due to the fact there was no provision in the budget for their salaries.   Five policewomen were being kept. The 15 policewomen, vowed to fight this action, taking it to the courts if necessary.

The four policewomen assigned to the Juvenile Court took action. They were Margaret Hildebrand, Emma Baker, Metta Davis and Nell Dunkle. On Wednesday the

29th, they employed an attorney to prepare a formal tort protesting their suspension.

Within days, all of the other policewomen had joined their suit: Anna Brunner, Elizabeth Denny, Irene Beyer, Bertha Duclus, Lillian Jaschka, Mary Cantlon, Anna Buck, Mary Moore, Mary Moriarty, Cozette Osborn and Sarah Rogers.

On December 29th, Chief of Police Claude F. Johnson stated the policewomen who will be dropped would be given a chance to resign December 31st.

If they did not, they would be suspended and formal charges would be preferred against them. He cited a recent court action which allowed him to drop recently hired policemen due to economic reasons.

The policewomen were afraid they would be charged with insubordination prior to winning their fight and wanted to keep their records clean.

Sergeant Rachel Schwier was demoted to policewoman and the board forcibly retired Sadie Osborn on the 29th.

The attorney for the policewomen, Ira M. Holmes, filed their complaint before Judge Harry O. Chamberlain in Circuit Court. He placed a temporary restraining order on Chief Johnson and the Board of Safety from discharging the policewomen, December 31, 1926.

The Judge set a hearing for next Monday, January 3, 1927. Defendants were named as Mayor John L. Duvall, members of the Board of Safety and Chief Johnson.

On January 8th, Judge Chamberlain issued a permanent injunction against the city from removing the policewomen. This was a victory for the women, who were ordered reinstated.

He told the women, "I can prevent you from being dismissed, but I can't stand sponsor for the collection of your wages." He recommended they file suit in court if the city did not pay them.   The 15 policewomen would not receive a salary for many months.

As would be learned in May, 1927, one of the policewomen working without pay had kept Chief Johnson informed about what was done and said at the policewomen's meetings.

Chief Claude F. Johnson ordered the 15 policewomen to undergo physical examinations on March 10, 1927. Johnson said this was not an unusual procedure and was necessary.

Boynton J. Moore of the city council, advised the women not to sign anything, since he suspected a trap. Meanwhile, Attorney Ira M. Holmes was planning to file suit against the city controller to transfer $28,000 to pay the policewomen's salaries for 1927.

Judge Byron K. Elliott of Superior Court Room 4 issued a writ of mandate, April 22, 1927, which ordered the city controller to pay the policewomen's salaries. It went to the State Supreme Court for judgement.

The judge commented, "as long as they are employed, they must be paid."

Chief Johnson called Detective Sarah Rogers into his office. Sarah was described in the news media as leading the policewomen in their struggle against the police department.

Johnson told her that she had "an unfriendly attitude toward him." He was going to remove her from the detective bureau and be assigned to dance hall inspection from 3 p.m. to 11 p.m.

Sarah Rogers stated afterward it was an "awful calling down" as she turned in her resignation, which Johnson accepted, May 7, 1927. She sued for back pay of $670.22 and other penalties amounting to $1,600.00 total, on May 10th.

On May 9, 1927, it was announced that Ira M. Holmes, attorney for the policewomen was starting a movement to get financial aid for them. He said he would start advertising in local newspapers, calling on citizens to contribute to a fund that would allow the policewomen to meet their financial responsibilities. They had received no pay since January 1st.

"There is no more justification in cutting off these women at the end of five years' service than there would be in cutting off the fire department by failure to make an appropriation", Mr. Holmes said. He further said he felt the administration merely wants to get rid of the women.

All of the 15 women had continued at their work, but several of them were in dire financial straits. On September 20, 1927, the new Chief, Claude M. Worley, recommended a plan to pay the policewomen $13,919 from a fund which contained money taken from suspended policemen's salaries and leaves of absence. Nothing came of this plan.

The Indiana Supreme Court on May 29, 1928 affirmed the decision of Marion County Superior Court, Room 4, holding that 20 Indianapolis policewomen were entitled to their salaries, as well as back pay, from the attempt to remove them from the force without trial before the Board of Safety. The women received their back pay.

Sadie Marzella Osborne was born July 19, 1888 Port Jefferson, Ohio to David L. Osborne and Marzella Jennie Warbington. She grew up in Indianapolis and received her education at Public School No. 33 and the Deaconess Home. She was a member of the Methodist Church. The deaconess' were active with the Methodist Hospital, Home for Aged Women and an outreach for immigrants, particularly Asians.

Left to right, Grace (24), Sadie (23) and Pearl (18) Osborne in December 1911. Photo courtesy of Barb LaFara.

In March 1912, Sadie Osborne was pastor's assistant at the Grace M.E. Church. She devoted a large part of her time to relieving the suffering of the poor in the neighborhood and trying to rescue wayward girls. She had recently rescued a young girl from a house of prostitution. This girl was then living with her grandparents in the country.

These were social skills that qualified her for the police work she would later do. She was still working at the Deaconess Home when the City of Indianapolis sought qualified females to be policewomen.

On May 2, 1918, on recommendation of Chief of Police George V. Coffin, the board of safety granted special police powers to Sadie Osborne and Blanch Vanness, who also was a deaconess at the Methodist Episcopal Church.

He said the women were detailed to the work of assisting and protecting young girls and women at Union Station. They had done valuable work at the depot for the past year through Travelers' Aid and were performing the work of policewomen. One week later, the first policewoman in

Indianapolis, Clara Burnside, was appointed and the city planned on appointing 10 women to work for her. Due to her fine work at Union Station, Sadie was a prime choice for the job.

When Sadie was appointed to the Indianapolis Police Department, June 15, 1918, she lived at 1102 North Beville Avenue on the east side.

Her background had been with the Methodist Deaconess Association in Indianapolis for nine years. Sadie took a three year course in social work at Kansas City.

Sadie's first assignment on July 2, 1918 was to attend to office duties at police headquarters. She was 5'4", 112 pounds when appointed.

Great-niece Barb LaFara tells that in the 1960's, the story told about Sadie was that "Aunt Sadie worked on the Vice Squad breaking up dice games at Union Station. While walking through the City Market, Sadie's sister told how Sadie worked in the market and watched for pick pockets and shoplifters. I imagined her as Angie Dickenson on 'Police Woman." Sadie's work on the "Morals Squad", as the Vice Squad was called, probably occurred in July 1919, when policewomen were employed to help the male officers.

Photograph of Sadie and her siblings, left to right: Pearl Jane Osborne LaFara, Sadie Osborne, Martha Grace Osborne Fithian, Rollin Osborne and Louis Osborne. This picture is undated, but is probably from about 1920. Photo courtesy of Barb LaFara.

She was assigned January 2, 1922 to become an investigator in the Juvenile Court. She did a lot of work to help the poor when working there.

Policewoman Sadie Osborne - 1921

---

[18] Official IPD portrait.

(Photo by Star Staff Photographer.)

PIGEON WITH THIRTY-NINE-INCH WING SPREAD.

The largest pigeon in the country is one of the features of the Indianapolis poultry show, now being given at Tomlinson hall. The bird was bought by W. P. Overman of Indianapolis, and arrived yesterday from California. The mammoth bird measures thirty-nine inches with wings spread. Miss Sadie Osborne, policewoman, is shown holding the pigeon.

February 8, 1923

In December 1924, Sadie was working in the detective division as an undercover shoplifting detective. She arrested a woman for stealing stockings on December 13th. "Family stories told about Aunt Sadie said

184

she worked vice cases and rescued girls from prostitution," said niece Barb LaFara.

Sadie Osborne retired December 29, 1926 from the Indianapolis Police Department.

Sadie died January 28, 1940 in Indianapolis of breast cancer. She was buried in Crown Hill Cemetery, Indianapolis, Indiana.

Bertha L. (Andrews) Duclus was born January 30, 1878 in Richland Center, Fulton County, Indiana to William and Jane (Babcock) Andrews. Her father was a farmer there in 1880. When she was 12, Bertha was working as a "shoe folder." By 1910, she was married to Willard Jesse

---

[19] Official IPD portrait, 1921.

Duclus, 40, who owned a grocery at 2957 McPherson Avenue in Indianapolis. Willard and Bertha lived at 3109 North Arsenal Avenue.

On October 15, 1910, a man snatched Bertha and a female friend's purses as they walked at 10 p.m. Neither was hurt. Bertha gave birth to a son William in 1913. He was her only child.

For several years, Bertha Duclus had given valuable assistance to the juvenile court in Marion County. This brought her to the attention of the Indianapolis Board of Safety Police when they made a decision to appoint 14 policewomen in 1918. They selected Bertha, who was issued badge #5.

After being sworn in, on July 2, 1918, Bertha and Policewoman Rena Reisner were partners, being assigned to Union Station and the Traction Terminal Station. Their shift was from 1:30 p.m. to 11:30 p.m.

They arrested a 17-year old girl for delinquency in June 1918 at the Southern Hotel, 232 South Illinois Street. In October,

Duclus, Reisner and Policewoman Anna
Buck sent home 32 girls, 15 women, 12 boys
and four men who shouldn't have been at
the stations. Numerous girls were also
arrested, so they were kept busy.

Bertha Duclus - 1918

Bertha Duclus personnel sheet.

Bertha was paired later with Sadie Osborne. While walking their beat looking for wayward girls on May 3, 1919, they saw a man named John Creek, 29, acting suspiciously around the intersection of West Washington Street and Capitol Avenue at night.

Lieutenant William Cox   Sergeant Fred Winkler

They stood and watched him. They saw him sell a half-pint of whiskey to a man. Since they were unarmed they used a police call box to call headquarters and Lieutenant William Cox and Sergeant Fred Winkler were sent to their assistance.

Creek tried to run from the policemen but they apprehended him and found a half pint of whiskey in his pocket. He was charged with violating the prohibition law.

Later that year, Bertha Duclus and Policewoman Margaret Hildebrand were assigned to the shoplift detail in downtown stores. They witnessed a man steal several articles from counters in the H.P. Wasson & Co. department store. He was arrested and sentenced to 20 days in jail, December 15, 1919.

Early on July 2, 1920, two girls, aged 15 and 13, alleged that two men sexually assaulted them during a car trip into Ohio. These men were arrested by Lieutenant Robert Woollen, Sergeant John Marren with Policewomen Duclus and Hildebrand.

On January 2, 1922, the department of policewomen was eliminated and several of the policewomen assigned to the IPD Detective Division under Inspector John Mullin. Bertha Duclus and Irene Beyer were made detectives and assigned to the undercover shoplifting detail. They continued to make arrests in this area.

When IPD decided to arm policewomen in March of 1922, Detectives Bertha Duclus and Irene Beyer went to the target range on June 29th. They made several bullseyes at twenty yards. They were using .32 revolvers and their shooting was considered comparable to the male detectives shooting.

Detective Duclus paired with Detective Sadie Osborne in 1923 to make shoplifting arrests. Their most exciting arrest occurred on October 18, 1923 at a 5 and 10 cent store downtown. They had a report two men were stealing articles from the counters. One man, Earl Gadd, age 21, saw the detectives and ran for the rear door.

The women followed and captured him and the other youth. They started for police headquarters with their prisoners. When they were in front of the Pettis Dry Goods Company, Gadd broke away and ran toward the revolving doors.

Detective Duclus followed and landed in the same area with Gadd. The revolving door kept going around and around until the suspect was thrown inside the store and Duclus, 5'8", 155 pounds, fell on top of him, still fighting.

While the fight was going on, John Gray, 21, the larger of the two men stood trembling in the custody of Miss Sadie Osborne (5'4" and 112 pounds). "I just grabbed my umbrella tight and prepared to stop him if he tried to break away," Detective Osborne said. "But he didn't. He just trembled." Exhausted, Earl Gadd was arrested. The men were charged with vagrancy.

In 1924, Duclus was paired with a new policewoman, Sarah Rogers. They were on shoplifting detail on December 23, 1924 when they saw a man acting suspiciously. The two female detectives were observing him and saw him put his hands in the coat pockets of a number of women without getting any money.

Bertha brushed up against him and put her hand in her pocket as if she was putting a pocketbook there. The man reached for her pocket and Duclus grabbed his arm, arresting him. Investigation showed he was part of a 3-man shoplifting ring that were in Indianapolis to ply their trade in the holiday crowds. They recovered stolen merchandise in their hotel room.

While working as a detective, Bertha Duclus probably made more arrests than any other policewoman.

On December 28, 1926, it was announced that the Board of Safety removed 15 policewomen from the department because there was only a provision in the 1927 budget for five.

Bertha Duclus was one of these 15 officers. Some of the policewomen sued the City of Indianapolis and a judge placed an injunction against the city, stopping the layoffs. However, the women worked without pay for all of 1927 before receiving back pay.

From 1928-1930, Bertha was a stolen vehicle records clerk.

Policewoman With Boyish Bob Hunts Missing Autos

Attire Confuses Those Visiting Department; Call Her 'Sir.'

[MARCH 9, 1928]

"Pardon me, sir, but is this the stolen automobile department?" some one asks at the window.

"Yes, it is. What can I do for you?" Policewoman Bertha Duclus, head of the department, looks up and asks.

"Why, I beg your pard—!" the person stammers as he shifts uneasily from one foot to the other.

Miss Duclus, her bobbed hair combed back in pompadour style, and wearing glasses, a man's shirt, tie and hat and a business suit, is mistaken for the male species at least five times each day.

Until she raises her head from her desk where she is busily at work or until she speaks, one cannot be blamed for addressing her as "sir," for looks are deceiving.

Miss Duclus, who has been head of her department for more than two years, takes care of all 'automobiles reported stolen, recovered or found abandoned. An average

Miss Bertha Duclus

of twenty cars literally pass through her department each day.

When an automobile is recovered or found abandoned and the owner is unknown, "Duke" checks the records in the Secretary of State's office in an effort to locate the owner.

When a car is reported stolen, she makes out a report which is read to all policemen at the three roll calls and they keep on the lookout for the stolen automobiles. When they locate the cars, she notifies the owners.

HAPGOOD SEEKS JOB

Will Stay in Coal Fields to Work and Speak.

By United Press

WILKES-BARRE, Pa., March 9.— Although leaders of the mine union faction which he so bitterly opposes may object, Powers Hapgood, Indi-

20

---

[20] 1928 article. IMPD Lichtenberger History Room.

IPD Detective Office, 1929. Left to right: Chief of Detectives Jerry Kinney, Lt. Herman Radamacher, Sgt. Harry Hillman, Sgt. Harry Connor, Ruth Schoen, Policewoman Cozette Osborn, Policewoman Bertha Duclus and Juanita Buttz.

By 1935, Bertha Duclus was working for the Juvenile Court as a police investigator. She and fellow investigator Hugh Dugan went to the address of William Pollard, 69, at 447 North Alabama Street on March 19, 1935. He had failed to appear in Juvenile Court on a charge of contributing to the delinquency of a 16-year old girl.

Bertha entered Pollard's apartment to find his body lying on a floor with a noose around his neck. He had hanged himself but someone had cut the body down. The body was taken to the morgue for further investigation.

The Indianapolis Police Department formed a new Crime Prevention Bureau for juvenile offenders on March 22, 1938. From now on, children who break the law will be brought here instead of the courts. The offices were on the second floor of police headquarters.

The new bureau would be headed by Sergeant Charles E. Weddle. His staff would include policewomen Nell Dunkle, chief assistant, Bertha Duclus and Emma Baker. Howard Hunt, social service worker, was also on the staff.

Bertha Duclus personnel sheet.

On December 7, 1939, Bertha was selected to be a delegate to the national convention of the Fraternal Order of Police, to be held in Phoenix, Arizona in 1940. The Juvenile Aid Division as it was now called in August 1941 was staffed by Sergeant Albert Magenheimer, three patrolmen and policewomen Metta Davis, Mary Moriarty and Bertha Duclus.

In 1943, during World War II, there was a manpower shortage. Policewomen for the first time since the 1920's were given more responsibility and patrolled the streets of Indianapolis. Veteran policewomen Anna Yoh and Bertha Duclus patrolled the bus and railroad stations, just as Bertha had done in 1918.

They did this now for the same reason, to question girls who appeared to be waiting for service men. In many cases they found the girls were runaways from other cities. They returned these girls to their homes.

While the majority of Mrs. Duclus' career was spent in Juvenile, she also worked in the stolen car division, keeping records.

She returned to the family home, in Fulton County, Indiana in 1944, after retiring from IPD with 26 years of service. She later moved to Rochester in Fulton County. They lived at 1510 Audubon Avenue there. Willard Duclus died May 12, 1951. Bertha was a member of the Trinity United Methodist Church there. She passed away

December 2, 1968 in Rochester. Burial was in the Richland Center IOOF Cemetery.

Lillian K. Jaschka was born July 15, 1883 in Indianapolis, Indiana to John and Catherine Jaschka. Her father was of

---

Russian-Polish descent and her mother was from Germany.

In 1900, the family lived at 767 West New York Street. Lillie as she was called at that time was a store clerk.

Lillian was a member of the United Methodist Church.

In 1910, Lillian Jaschka was living with her half-brother Jacob Kurtz at 767 West Market Street. Jacob was then a detective with the Indianapolis Police Department.

Lillian became a County Jail matron in 1914. During World War I, Lillian started a "sewing bee" in the jail, in which the female inmates made about 20-30 "fracture pillows" a day. These pillows were sent to military hospitals in France.

Lillian was one of the 14 policewomen appointed by the Board of Safety on June 15, 1918. She said she joined because two of her brothers were already on the department. The aforementioned Jacob "Jake" Kurtz was one of the best known detectives in the west and had died in 1915 after 27 years with IPD. At the time of the appointment, Lillian lived at 28 South Alabama Street, which was next door to police headquarters at 35 South Alabama Street.

Lillian Jaschka was assigned on July 2, 1918 to be Matron in the City Jail at police headquarters. She was here through 1926. She was another one of the policewomen "laid off" in December 1926 due to no funds being available to pay their 1927 salary. She also ended up staying with IPD after a lawsuit was settled.

On November 1, 1926, Lillian Jaschka was not a matron and apprehended a runaway at a motion picture theater at Capitol and Washington Streets. She was partnered with Policewoman Anna Buck. She was promoted to Matron again, December 29, 1931.

Lillian spent 10 years on "street duty", and then worked in the IPD Record Room taking telephone complaints. She was considered a good shot.

"After 20 years one learns to take things as they come. I'm a plain woman and call a spade a spade. I don't let them bluff me", she said in 1939. She drove her own car, owned a pet troy fox terrier and liked to raise flowers.

Policewoman Lillian Jaschka

Lillian in 1939.

She retired in 1944. Lillian was a member
of the Naomi Chapter, Order of the Eastern
Star and the Fraternal Order of
Policewomen. She was then living at 3026
East 10th Street. Lillian died of diabetes,
May 7, 1953, in Indianapolis. She is buried
in Crown Hill Cemetery.

Isobel (Bonebrake) Phillips was born December 25, 1868 in Rockville, Indiana to Andrew J. Bonebrake and Lydia Catherine Robertson. On August 22, 1886 in Parke County, Indiana, Isabel married George Phillips. She used the Isabel spelling as an adult.

From 1910-1918, Isabel Phillips had been a nurse in charge of the hospital at the Indiana Girls School in Clermont, Indiana.

She had gained much experience in dealing with girls and women there. This was experience that the Board of Safety valued when choosing her to be one of the first policewomen in Indianapolis. Issued badge number 13, she was assigned as Matron in the City Prison on July 2, 1918.

In 1920, Isabel Phillips was living at 420 North LaSalle Street. On February 2, 1920, Mrs. Rachel Johnson, 24, attempted suicide by jumping into a lagoon at Garfield Park. The water had ice on it. A passerby pulled her out of the water.

Motor Policemen John G. Moriarty and Frank Reilly took the woman to headquarters, where Isabel Phillips, police matron took off the Rachel's wet clothes and wrapped her in blankets. Isabel then called the woman's husband, who had reported her missing.

Mayor Lou Shank wanted to put policewomen on beats across town when he took office, January 3, 1922. Isabel Phillips, who had no previous experience outside of being a matron, had been given a beat to walk at night by herself on the southeast side of Indianapolis. She walked her beat that night and didn't have any unusual experiences but if it hadn't been for the exposure (cold weather), she would have stuck with it. Instead, she submitted her resignation, which was accepted by the Board of Safety, January 4, 1922.

Isabel's son Clarence A. Phillips (1887-1954) served as a Captain in the U.S. Army during WWI. He moved to San Francisco, California after the war and Isabel joined him there.

Isabel bought a home worth $14,000 at 1260 York Street there and began working as a nurse again, in a hospital. She took a cruise to Honolulu, March 6, 1934 on the S.S. Mariposa. She was still working as a nurse. By 1940 she was retired. Her sister Katherine Wulf was now living with her.

Isabel Phillips died in 1956 and is buried next to her sister in Cypress Lawn

Memorial Park cemetery, Colma, San Mateo
County, California.

Isabel Phillips, 1921

Mary Ena Roberts was born January 3,
1856 in Salem, Washington County,
Indiana. Her parents were John Roberts, a

free African-American and Mariah (Roberts) Roberts, part free African-American, part Cherokee Native American. According to a January 31, 1943 *Indianapolis Star* article, the Cherokee ancestry descends from a chief named Red Bird. Red Bird lived from 1721 to 1820.

The family resided near Salem in 1860. Mary's father was not in the household, apparently being deceased. The family moved to Bedford, in Lawrence County, Indiana about 1862.

On September 5, 1863 in Bedford, Mary's mother Mariah remarried to a man named Thomas F. Crossen (1843-1904). Mary used the last name of Crossen after that. Thomas Crossen joined the 28th United States Colored Troops, Company C, on December 31, 1863. He was promoted to Corporal, January 4, 1864. He mustered out November 8, 1865 at Corpus Christi, Texas.

Mary left the family about 1877 and settled in Indianapolis, Indiana. On September 13,

1877 in Indianapolis, she married Philip Mays. She had a daughter named Lucille born in July 28, 1878.

On June 10, 1880, the census taker recorded Philip and Mary Mays living in Indianapolis. They resided at 226 West Vermont Street. Philip was a janitor in a bank, Mary was keeping house.

On January 2, 1882, she and Emma Christy were among the women who helped out at an open house at the Bethel AME Church on Vermont Street in Indianapolis.

The Bethel African Methodist Episcopal Church - 1918

On January 24, 1885, gave birth to a son, Garrold Edward Mays. Mary E. Mays worked for a number of years for the Flower Mission of Indianapolis, an organization that existed to bring flowers to hospital patients but also to help the poor and unfortunate.

In 1884, the work of the Mission had outgrown what volunteers could handle and Mary Mays was appointed as district nurse to find patients who needed help. They asked her to conduct research on the needs of the visitors to the city dispensary. Mary found that most patients lacked knowledge on how to care for the sick.

During her tenure with the Flower Mission, Mary Mays never was an official member. It isn't known if this was due to her status as the only known woman of color to serve.

For the next 20 years Mays served as a visiting nurse with the Flower Mission and became very familiar to the citizens of Indianapolis. In 1892, she and Philip Mays were divorced. He died in 1895.

Mary Mays had a relationship of some kind with Horace Heston. Both were called into court on August 23, 1895 after a disturbance in which Heston was fined for assault and battery upon Mary. Heston was a former police officer who was reputed to be a gambling king in Indianapolis.

Lucile Mays, only daughter of Mary E. Mays, led an accomplished life herself. She attended school in Indianapolis, and then took a course in the preparatory school of Howard University, Washington D.C. She then completed a course in the nurses' training school at the Freedman's Hospital in Washington. It was a teaching hospital for the Howard University Medical School.

In 1900, Mary resided with her children at 621 Blackford Avenue on the west side of Indianapolis. Her daughter Lucile had returned from Washington and was now a nurse herself.

The church that Lucile attended, the Bethel A.M.E. Church, held an election for state officers. Members of the Sewing Circle were candidates. Lucile ran for Secretary of State on the Prohibition Party ticket. She was defeated by Ada Goines. This was a "campaign" held for fun and to raise money.

Another visiting nurse for the Flower
Mission in 1907. Is this Lucile Mays?

Lucile returned to Indianapolis where she
assisted her mother in caring for charity

patients. She married on August 15, 1908 to Dr. Walter T. Bailey.

Walter Bailey was born August 28, 1885 in New Castle, Indiana to Edward and Carrie Bailey. He graduated from Walden University and Meharry Medical College in Nashville, Tennessee.

Lucile volunteered for the Sisters of Charity and served as chairman of the auditing committee in 1912.

Mary was reappointed to the Flower Mission as a District Nurse annually and it was noted when she was appointed August 2, 1902 that she was the only African-American employee of the Mission.

At a Board of Directors Meeting of the Flower Mission on May 21, 1903, they said that Mary Mays was "Good for Man and Beast" after she took care of a horse whose throat had been viciously cut. Mary sewed and dressed the wound.

On July 28, 1903, at 720 West 11th Street, lived a 16-year old African-American girl named Henrietta Smith. Henrietta was afflicted with what was described as a strange disease, in actuality, tubercular decay of the joints of her left leg. She had been bedridden for 17 months.

Nurse Mary Mays had been concerned about this girl for quite a while and had been directly in charge of her care for four months. Mary had spent much energy trying to make Henrietta's life easier.

The mother, Mrs. Smith, who was told, this was a hopeless case. Her church pastor, Reverend Charles Johnson told the mother that unless her daughter was baptized she could not enter the Kingdom of Heaven and blamed the mother for the lingering illness from not washing the girl's sins away years ago.

After lengthy conversations about this with her mother, Henrietta apparently became enthusiastic about the idea of being baptized. She set a time of 6 p.m. Tuesday, July 28th for the ceremony. She then called Mary Mays.

Upon learning of the proposed baptism on July 27th, Mary did everything in her power to block the parents' plans. She told the mother that that such an action would result in the immediate death of the daughter, as she was not strong enough to withstand the shock of being completely submerged in water.

Refusing to consent to the removal of the girl from the home, Mary threatened to have the girl's mother arrested. She then called police headquarters to see if they could stop the baptism.

Mrs. Smith reacted indignantly, saying she would have the ceremony performed at any cost. The plan now changed to have the ceremony done in the home. Two African-American ministers arrived, along with one hundred or more of his flock. Two leading members of the 2nd Colored Baptist Church carried a porcelain bath tub into the sick room, next to Henrietta's bed.

The ministers, Rev. Charles Johnson and a Mr. Wilson, went ahead. Just moving

Henrietta one inch caused her to scream from pain and faint. They had to double the girl up to get her fully under the water. Henrietta experienced excruciating pain when she was touched and screamed loudly. Reverend Johnson quit at this point, but Mr. Wilson pressed on, Henrietta's shrieks being heard throughout the neighborhood.

Since she lived one block away, Mary Mays heard the screams and saw the commotion of neighbors reacting to them. A large, excited crowd gathered around the house. After the 2nd attempt, at this point, Nurse Mary Mays came into the room and interrupted the proceedings. She had some things to say and wasn't holding back.

"You are committing murder. I just called for the police to come and stop this baptism, which I believe will result in the death of Henrietta." Then, Mary told Pastor Johnson, the mother and the assembled congregation not to follow this course.

Within minutes, several of the older members of the congregation started to shake their heads in disapproval of the baptism. The women began to talk among themselves.

Reverend Johnson at this point addressed the brethren and said the girl was not ready for this and it might be a good idea to wait a day or so.

While he spoke, Mary Mays worked with the girl to bring her back to consciousness. The crowd of people slowly walked out of the house. After the ordeal, Mary Mays told a reporter for the *Indianapolis Journal*.

"What Henrietta has endured the last few weeks would have killed any ordinary mortal", Mary said. She then related a story of how the mother had taken $15 sent to her by her son for his sister's care and spent $10 of it on a fake medicine man.

She spent the remaining $5 on paying for a pallbearer's carriage to carry Henrietta and another girl sick with rheumatism to see the charlatan. Mary had been busy the past week or so trying to care for the two girls, who had just about recovered from the agonizing ride to see the medicine man.

Henrietta passed away the evening of Sunday, August 2nd.

Before this however, Mary Mays was already involved in another case where mercy was needed. A man named John Reed had died at the City Hospital. On July 31, 1903, Mary came to the hospital and after asking for his clothes, found that they were very soiled from the dirt he was digging in when he died.

As the schedule for the burial made no time to ask his friends for clothing for the body, Mary suggested a winding sheet. Together, Mary and Mrs. Landers of the Home of the Friendless, accompanied the heartbroken wife to Mount Jackson cemetery. They comforted her and her two children and tried afterward to arrange for their future welfare. The family was poverty stricken.

In September of 1903, a typhoid fever epidemic was raging in Norwood, an African-American settlement on the southeast side of Indianapolis. Twenty-one cases of typhoid had been reported and sanitary conditions in the area were pretty bad.

The Indianapolis News, the local paper started a program in 1903 to provide free pasteurized milk to children at different agencies. Among these was the Flower Mission.

Speaking on behalf of the agency, Mary Mays stated, "The milk is a splendid thing. It should be given to well babies as soon as they are weaned. After the germs of disease have a chance to spread through the system, the trouble has been done. Then it is generally too late even by feeding pure milk to stop the sickness. To keep the babies from bowel trouble in hot weather, the pasteurized milk should be given them from the start. I shall be glad to have the milk for some of my cases."

Being outside the Indianapolis city limits, these people, who were very poor, had no public assistance. The flower Mission was notified on September 9th of the situation. That afternoon, Nurse Mary Mays was dispatched to Norwood and looked in on the family of Clarence Shirley, African-American.

When Mary entered the residence, she was "appalled" at the conditions. Clarence Shirley, his wife, aged mother and two children lived in two rooms and all but one was sick with typhoid. Mary related later to an Indianapolis News reporter, "It was a shocking sight and a more dreadful condition of things I have never found in my experience."

The family was crowded in two beds. A six-year old daughter was the only family member not ill and she was caring for the rest of the family. "Think of a child of six years trying to nurse five typhoid fever patients!" Mary said. Realizing that ice was crucial to the treatment, the little girl went to the railroad several times each day to gather up pieces of ice that had fallen from cars.

Mary Mays found the temperature of the parents was 106 and 104. The house was very hot and almost unbearable. The Flower Mission sent clean bedding to the home. Dr. Samuel Furnas, an African-American Indianapolis physician, provided free care.

The Flower Mission assigned Mary to duty at the City Hospital on November 1, 1903. She was there all day.

Mary Mays was sent to the home of George Harold and wife in the middle of January, 1904. They were living in an old box car. Their baby had just died.

On January 17th, Mary said to the *Indianapolis Star*, "I propose to make George Harold and his wife just as happy in their little old box car as the happiest people in Indianapolis. I will go out there tomorrow with a wagon load of furniture for the little house and some warm clothes and before we are through, they will live like humans again." Mary continued, "The car will be a good, warm home for them, as soon as I find some builders' paper for the walls. I wish the Star would ask someone to give me some."

Mary knew that Harold wasn't lazy. "One thing I noticed the first time I saw him was that his overalls were worn out in front, from work, and not behind, from sitting down too much."

The following day, the Star reported that Mary Mays' appeal had brought results. President Fisher of the Capital Paper Company sent a letter to the Star saying they could have the necessary material. When told of the letter, Mary became enthusiastic and will at once procure it and have the "room" papered.

Another of the cases Mary was called in on was that of Eliza Collins, who was described as sick and insane. She was living in "squalid" conditions and told Mary she refused to go to an institution. Mary called physicians into the case, who declared her insane and had her taken to the Jullietta

Hospital for Incurables on January 18, 1904.

On January 25, 1904, Mary was notified of another insane woman who set her house on fire on January 19th. Mary said the relatives would be asked to care for the woman before they tried to put her in an institution.

There was a flooding situation developing on the west side of Indianapolis while Mary was dealing with the insane woman. Due to freezing weather, creeks in the Jackson Park neighborhood had spilled out of their banks and froze over.

Mary Mays and a man helped a Mr. Brunson carry his wife and baby through the flood. They waded from the home near 25th Street. The Brunson house had flooded on the night of January 21st and they had to flee to a neighbor's home. The Brunson family was ill from exposure.

The worst flood in Indianapolis history up to then, occurred on March 26, 1904. The flood occurred in the neighborhood of

Indiana Avenue and Fall Creek. Twenty-five acres of land west of Fall Creek near Indiana Avenue and 10th Street were under water by morning.

Indianapolis Police became aware of the situation when an African-American woman walked into headquarters downtown at 1 a.m. and said her home was full of water and she had no place to go. Police then learned many people in that area were calling for help.

City police found a large flat bottomed boat and an old river man named Hasselberg. He understood the currents better than the officers and he piloted it to the barn of the old "pesthouse", where the William Lauterback family was imprisoned. Mr. Lauterback was 45, blind and disabled. He was rescued along with his wife and five children.

The boat went two blocks down stream and then hit a snag in the middle of Fall Creek, which almost threw the occupants out. A large hole was torn in the bottom of the boat, which began filling with water. They quickly made for the shore. This was the 1500 block of Hiawatha Street.

Just before 4 p.m. that day, an aqueduct carrying water of the canal across Fall Creek collapsed with a crash heard for many blocks. The collapse of the aqueduct spilled the water of the canal into the flooded area, sending water into the bottom lands. Hundreds of people were forced to leave their homes. Again, the Lauterback family found themselves in a flooded home.

Late in the afternoon, Mary Mays, her daughter Lucile and a niece, Mrs. Claude Walker went to aid the residents. Water was up to the hub of the vehicle they rode in. They rescued William Lauterback, his wife and five children. Then with the assistance of a man named Collins, Mary and her family rescued sixty additional people.

A total of 400 persons were driven from their homes. The Indianapolis Journal described Mary's actions as a "brave rescue." Sadly, William Lauterback died on September 13, 1904.

Arrow indicates where Mary Mays rescued William Lauterback.

Mary Mays was always ready to celebrate the United States of America in a patriotic way. An occasion came on Sunday, July 3, 1904 at the Epworth League of Hall Place Methodist Episcopal Church. She and other woman gave recitations for the holiday.

Mary Mays reported on June 30, 1904 that the pasteurized milk sent by the

Indianapolis News to typhoid fever patients had done "inestimable good." Patients fed the milk were gaining from ¼ to 1 pound a day.

In August of 1904, Mary Mays came across a sight common in today's world, a married couple totally addicted to morphine and cocaine. Dr. Kidd and his wife were living in the Oakley hotel in a pitiful state. Mary took charge of this case and succeeded in making arrangements with the City Hospital to take the woman in and let her work to pay for her care.

Unfortunately, while she could be cured, she and the husband would not be separated and consumed enough morphine and cocaine in two days to kill 30 men not already addicted to the drugs. Worse, Mary Mays was faced with paying their hotel bill or they will be thrown into the street. Dr. Kidd had pawned all of his wife's clothes to purchase drugs.

Mary Mays found no rest or respite from the appalling conditions to be found in

Indianapolis in 1904. On August 20th, she found another tuberculosis case. "In the rear of 42 South Oriental Street", Mary said, "I found a woman alone in the last stages of consumption. Her husband had been discouraged because he could find no place to take her and had left. Her name is Mrs. Herschel Thrusher."

Mary continued, "The department for incurable women in the Flower Mission is full and I have been taking care of the poor woman as best I could, hoping that there would soon be a vacancy. The neighbors are all afraid of the disease and the woman lies for hours without attention. She told me that her husband had become angry and had torn his picture from the wall."

Every week Mary faced another case of sickness, poverty and degradation, too numerous to detail here. How she persevered working alone for the most part, is unknown.

Mary wanted to develop a way of instilling charity in the mind of children. She hosted an event for the Mother Goose Club, made up of African-American children aged 8 to 14 years of age. She had the children piece together quilts to be furnished to the poor. Entertainment was provided on November 22, 1904 to raise money to furnish a Christmas dinner for poor African-American children. Many people attended. The children wore costumes representing Mother Goose characters.

The party Mary Mays raised money for was held in her home at 616 West 11th Street, December 26, 1904. Arrangements were made for 50 African-American children but before it was over, 89 children came.

The children were given a royal treatment at dinner and each was given a beautiful gift. Mary had decorated her dining room with Christmas greenery. A large bell hung above the table.

A "Santa Claus" handed out the gifts. A manger and Star of Bethlehem were in a downstairs room. The Christmas Story was told by a pastor of Simpson Chapel. Mary had a large white "camel" standing next to the manger.

In 1904, Mary Mays, district nurse attended 769 cases and made 2,205 visits to the sick. Among these were 76 cases of scarlet fever, which occurred during a local epidemic. She also handled 75 cases of typhoid fever during another epidemic. Mary nursed 125 cases of tuberculosis.   This was twice the number handled by the other Flower Mission nurses in Indianapolis.

One of the cases Nurse Mary Mays dealt with in 1905 was that of Billie Jones. Mary found the Jones family after a long search. In the month of December, she found the shanty, built on a hill over a river. Mrs. Jones and her son Billie lived there.

As Mary approached the home, she saw the mother on her hands and knees, hands warped from rheumatism, scraping up coal leavings from the snow. Mary knelt by her side and began helping her find the coal scraps. Billie, the woman's adopted son, had tuberculosis of the hip joint, from which he suffered great pain.

Both had been looked after by the Flower Mission for years. Billie lay in bed, thin and pale but cheerful. The old woman who took care of him had torn shoes and her clothing wasn't suited for the winter weather.

Mary Mays said "It is a real pleasure to labor for Billie Jones and his mother. There is no heaviness or drudgery in working for their welfare and comfort. Would there were more such sunny souls in the world. The wealthy as well as the wretched might learn sweet lessons of endurance and patience in the little shanty on the bluff where Mother Jones cares night and day for her Billie."

In 1905, Mary Mays gave her opinion as to what was needed in local health care. "Smallpox is looked after the year round. There is a place set off for the smallpox patient. This is right. It is proper to keep down the spread of the disease. But the city and county have no safeguard against the consumptive. Tuberculosis infection is disregarded. The infected must ride upon the street cars and go about freely in the public places. They must work in the company of others as long as they are able to stand. They can do no better. They have no place where they can be taken for a cure in the early stages of the disease. They have no place where they may be treated. It is our opinion that every person, rich or poor, should have the same treatment for tuberculosis. The tuberculosis patient should have good, pure, nourishing food, pure milk first of all; clean, well-ventilated rooms, clean beds and light, warm bedding. All this costs money."

The Flower Mission opened up a 25-bed unit for TB patients in 1903, but it was for White people only. Marion County would not allocate funds for the treatment of African-American people with TB until 1919.

Mary resided at 616 West 11th Street in 1905. She was one of two known African-American nurses in the city of Indianapolis then. When Mary submitted her annual report for 1905, on January 20, 1906, she recorded that she made 33,329 visits, 269 being African-American people and nursed 9,090 people.   Horace Heston, age 53, died at Mary's home on West 11th Street, in September 1906. His wife and son died about two years ago, when he had become an invalid. Mary had taken care of him.

Mary E. Mays – Angel of Indianapolis

Mary's humanitarianism became evident to the world on March 14, 1907. She was riding in a street car on Indiana Avenue at 10 a.m. that morning. She was returning from treating a patient. Seated in the front of the car, she saw a dog lying on the street car track on its side. As the car approached, the dog raised its head but the motorman didn't attempt to stop.

She then ran to the glass door opening into his compartment. "Stop this car at once or I will come in there and make you!" shouted Mary, bringing many of the passengers of the car to their feet in amazement.

The car began rocking wildly at the corner of St. Clair and West Streets as it ran over the dog. As soon as the car stopped, Mary Mays leapt from the front of the car and darted toward the fender.

She then pulled the dog from underneath it, whose hind legs had been completely severed by the street car. Carrying it in her arms, she staggered to the curb and sat there, while more and more blood drenched her gown. Tears came down her eyes as she wept and begged bystanders to notify the humane officer at the police station.

Mary's dress was ruined. When the Indianapolis Police humane officers arrived, she assisted them in taking the animal where it could be humanely put down. She then joined in a protest giving the name of the motorman on her car to the secretary of the Street Railway Company.

On September 1, 1907, a religious fanatic named William Kirby, who advertised himself with handbills as the pastor of the "Church of Christ", went on a violent spree. The Indianapolis Police Department received a call of a man cutting his wife at 1114 Brook Street in the late afternoon.

IPD Bicycle men William Wilson and Gollnisch started for the location. Before they arrived, Patrolman Irick heard of the trouble and ran to the home. He found Kirby attacking his wife with a long butcher knife, trying to cut some of her clothing off.

Irick came to her aid, pulling his revolver, causing a standoff with Kirby. A moment later, the two bicyclemen appeared in the room, causing Kirby to become enraged.

They used their nightsticks on Kirby but he managed to stab Patrolman Wilson in the chest with his knife. The blade struck the breast bone, bent and then broke.

Gollnisch knocked the remaining part of the knife out of Kirby's hand and a fight began between the three officers and the suspect. Wilson didn't realize he was stabbed until after the fight was over. Kirby had been released from the workhouse a short while earlier after serving a long term for beating a man almost to death.

In the aftermath of Kirby's rampage, Mary Mays was quoted as saying, "Twice I called the police myself and told them that Kirby should not be allowed to run free. He had his room fixed up as a religious temple with a white altar in the center and residents of the neighborhood really feared that he would attempt to sacrifice some of their children upon this altar."

She continued, "He would appear on the street corners arrayed in a long white robe and preach. Neighbors were afraid of him and they as well as myself reported him to the police. Each time that I reported, the desk sergeant said he would investigate but it seems that nothing was done."

On Christmas Day, 1907, Mary Mays gave a dinner and Christmas tree to about 200 poor African-American children of her neighborhood. She also had quite a number of other children as guests of honor.

A true story of the Christmas spirit occurred in Indianapolis during the holiday season of 1907, thanks to Mary Mays. She found a family of four where the bread-winner was the 14-year old daughter. Mary visited this family on December 23, 1907.

Mary declined to give out the family's name but did tell the local media that "This family needs clothing as well as other things and I hope that somebody will see that its urgent needs are supplied. This is the Christmas giving time and I know of no other place where such gifts would be more properly placed that with this family."

Mary continued, "The father is dying with a cancer of the face. His life can last only a short time longer. The mother, who formerly was employed in one of the downtown stores and who is a good woman, is required to care for him and cannot go out to do work."

"This is a deserving family if ever there was one and I hope that somebody will take an interest in the members and give them some clothes and provisions. The family has never received a cent's worth of charity from any source."

Within minutes of the *Indianapolis News* carrying this story, calls of help began coming into Mary Mays. This continued through December 26th. A total of 61 calls came in. As related by Mary Mays herself –

"The result was wonderful. One man called me and told me to take the boy to a clothing store and fit him out with a complete outfit of new clothing. I got this for him Tuesday night (Christmas Eve)."

Mary continued, "Another man gave him a pair of shoes. Another offered a suit to be delivered today. Another well-known man said he would take the boy under his care and place him in a conservatory of music and train his voice. Then a coal dealer called and said he would send out a load of coal. Others sent groceries, fruit, candies and all sorts of provisions that would help to make Christmas mean something to that family."

However, Mary mentioned one still existing need. "There is still one thing to be done. The little girl has been employed and has been earning $4 a week, on which the family has subsisted, but after this week she will be out of work and the slender income will cease. I hope that someone will come forward with a place for her to work and with some clothing for her to wear. I wish the little girl would be looked after. She is a good girl and now is the time to do something for her. The poor mother wept as she poured out her thanks for all that had been done for them."

Mary purchased a lot measuring 25x168 feet located on the north side of 11th Street, west of West Street, in January 1908, for $2,000.00. The address was 1041 North West Street. She moved to this address.

Mary was called to 221 North Alabama Street the evening of February 5, 1908 on a man starving to death. He was Dr. Nathan Fritz, 73 years of age. He had grown old, lost his wife and home and when he became ill, found a small room and was slowly starving to death. This was a planned suicide.

Mary found that the Board of Public Safety and the Board of Health didn't want to get involved in the case. Through the Flower Mission, Mary made arrangements to have him taken to the City Hospital, where he was made warm and comfortable.

Mary Mays' workload became so great that a call for help was made by the Flower Mission on February 21, 1908. They put out a call for additional nurses. In addition to caring for many babies, at this time she was caring for a number of paralyzed people, eleven cancer cases and 125 cases of tuberculosis. Thirty-five new TB cases were reported and looked after by Mary in the past week.

It was revealed that Mary Mays, in her visits, uses about 300 street car tickets a month, about 100 of which were furnished by the Traction and Terminal Company.

Dealing with so many sick people, it was inevitable that Mary herself would fall ill. This happened in early June, 1909. She slowly was recovering from an attack of typhoid fever.

Mary Mays planned many parties and usually was responsible for the decorations. One such event was held June 9, 1910 at the Douglass School, No. 19. She supervised the costuming.

Mary and her children lived at 616 West 11th Street in 1910. Lucile worked at the Post Office, Gerrold as a newspaper printer.

Early in this century, upper-class African-American families in the Midwest began to request a "Negro summer resort" in Benton Harbor, Michigan. It was advertised in 1910 as the "Atlantic City of the Race" and included bathing facilities and privately owned cottages.

Mary left Indianapolis August 21, 1910 for 10 days at the West Michigan Resort. She took her children Gerrold and Lucile and the trip became an annual event for Mary.

In October 1910, a number of ladies met at Lincoln Hospital for the purpose of organizing a ladies' auxiliary. The organization was formed for the purpose of assisting in the work of the Hospital. Mary Mays was elected president.

To promote the education of new nurses, Mary held a party at her home in November 1910. Proceeds would be for the benefit of the Lincoln Hospital Training School. Her sister-in-law Mrs. Charles Crossen and daughter Lucile were hostesses.

Mary Mays the district nurse spent Christmas Day, 1910 visiting the sick and needy, distributing bundles containing fruits toys and candies. Forty-two children were made happy by these presents from the "Sunshine Club". The Flower Mission made a decision to add another Visiting Nurse to help Mary Mays, the only nurse making the rounds, on February 7, 1911.

Mary Mays and her siblings attempted to be admitted to the Cherokee Nation as members of the tribe. This request was rejected April 19, 1911 as there was no evidence of their family on the 1835 list of tribal members.

Mary Mays and Georgia Nance were sent in May 1911 as delegates to a "Colored Women's Club Federation" state meeting at Marion, Indiana by the Lincoln Hospital Auxiliary. In August of 1911, Mary and her daughter Lucile left for a two-week vacation at the West Michigan Resort.

Lucile left Indianapolis in August 1912 to join her husband Walter in Shelbyville, Tennessee. He had a successful medical practice there.

Mary was called into Juvenile court on May 6, 1913. She testified that Frank Smith, of 242 North Oakland Street, struck his little girl on the ear with a hammer and had mistreated his other children and his sick wife. The man was sentenced to six months in the workhouse. In September of that year, she also was involved in a case where a man was sentenced to the workhouse for 6 months for contributing to the delinquency of a 15-year old girl.

Lucile Mays Bailey, died in November 1913 at the age of 32 of double pneumonia, at her home in Springfield, Tennessee. Her body was brought to Indianapolis for burial in Crown Hill. She had been ill for four days. Her husband Walter moved to Marion, Indiana where he was a practicing physician until 1942 and died in 1950. The funeral was held at Mary Mays' home at 1041 North West Street.

Mary's remaining child, Garrold, moved to Los Angeles, California by 1914. He married a woman named Harriett Pritchet and was working as an auto mechanic.

For a charity ball held in November of 1913 for the benefit of the Flower Mission, Mary Mays wrote a sketch to illustrate some of the calls made on her as the nurse of the Mission:

"First, a phone call from police headquarters in a big and kindly voice: 'Nurse, we have a boy down here who is very badly crippled. He was found sleeping out in the sleep at night. Will you look after him? The reply is always 'yes.'

"Another call is: 'Mr. B. wants you to come right away; bring some bandages and salve and dress his leg.'

"At the sound of the telephone bell again, a timid little voice is heard over the wire: 'Please come and bathe my sick paps.' There is a rap at the door. It is a neighbor of a very sick woman with a lot of children, and her husband has gone away and left her

without food or coal. 'Will you come and help her?' is the request.

"Another calls: 'There is a lady mighty sick over here and she wants to go to the hospital.'

"At the break of day there is a distressing call at the door: 'Nurse, nurse, come quick and see how John has beat my daughter Ann over the head with the skillet.' And another, 'My husband left me with five children and the baby is so sick and the other children have nothing to eat. Will you help us a little?'

"The baby comes whether prepared for or not and in many cases it is unprepared for. Three cases of the kind came this week. In one of these the mother was in a dark, damp cellar, on a cot of rags, the baby's bed was a dilapidated trunk.

"In the south part of town in an old house, was an old woman and her only companion was a dog. Soap and water were strange to them. The woman was seriously ill. She must be cared for. A policeman, called by a *neighbor, was afraid to brave the dirt. The room was filled with every kind of vermin and the woman was laid on a clean blanket in the yard until the ambulance came. Did she die? Of course, she did.*

"These and more are the cases of a single week. Helpless and hopeless conditions were everywhere, but the Flower Mission is the lighthouse of hope to bring poor people to care and kindness until they grow well or until the end comes."

The week of January 14, 1914, Mary supervised 25 new nursing cases taken up by the Flower Mission. Perhaps exhausted from this and the recent death of her daughter, Mary planned to leave soon for a two-month vacation in California. While there she intended to make an investigation of hospital and nursing work.

A parade designed to help start a campaign to fight germs and disease went through the streets of Indianapolis on October 2, 1914. The parade started at 3 p.m. on North Meridian Street, being led by a car carrying the Chief of Police Samuel Perrott and other police officials. One of the largest floats was that of the Indianapolis Flower Mission. The theme was that of two life savers in a canoe saving a victim drowning in a sea of disease. Riding on the float were six women, including Mrs. Mary Mays.

Mary Mays was elected District Nurse of the Flower Mission on February 6, 1915. Mary gave an address on May 16, 1915 at Simpson Chapel. She gave another one titled "Safety First and Health" on March 5, 1916 at the Second Christian Church. Mary was continually attempting to promote good health habits.

A meeting of the local branch of the National League for the Betterment of Urban Conditions among Colored People, recently organized, was held April 6, 1916 at the African-American Y.M.C.A. Mary Mays was among the speakers.

She spoke on general conditions in the African-American community. She said one of the most important needs was a paid probation officer for African-American delinquents. A committee was appointed to investigate in relation to this issue.

An executive committee was appointed with Mary Mays among the leading citizens the members.

In August of 1916, Mary found a 14-year old African-American girl, in the last stages of TB, deserted in a rooming house where she lived with an aunt. She was penniless. Unable to find a home for her, Mary obtained permission to take the girl to the city hospital for a few days and continued to try and find a home for her. This highlighted a problem in the city for African-American people suffering from tuberculosis who had no place to live.

The Indianapolis News published a story on October 19, 1916 about the many labors of Nurse Mary Mays. She had been beginning to show the strain of using shoe leather to visit all of her patients. A group of her admirers had begun a fund to purchase an automobile for her to ease her duties. The story described Mrs. Mays as a familiar figure in the streets of Indianapolis. "She wore a blue habit, the long blue veil streaming from her small bonnet across her shoulders." The story ended this way: "What Mrs. Mays deserves is a car of gold."

There was a report on October 20, 1916 that in the past 21 years with the Flower Mission, Mary Mays had made 65,000 calls, at all hours of the day or night.

Plans were announced on November 18, 1916 to give the automobile to Mary Mays on Thanksgiving Day. John Shine, veteran Indianapolis Police Officer, attached to the Juvenile department, had the following to say about Mary Mays.

John Shine

"For more than twenty years this woman has trudged through snow and sleet, through rain and sunshine, to care for the sick poor. I have long been a police officer in Indianapolis and I have seen her. Why, man, I have seen that little woman enter homes that I would not enter on risk of losing my badge. All the filth that ever laid in human path was before her – yet in she went to battle for a baby's life. Through the long hours of the night she fought it out, and the next day, she told me that she had walked home, a distance of three miles, through zero weather, in the hope of cleansing herself of the vermin that clung to her garments.

"Should a woman like that have an automobile in order to save her faltering feet? Should she? Why, man, she should have a dozen of them if the people of this community hoped, even in a measure, to repay her for the work she has done.

"Through alley and hovel she has gone at all hours of the night, a lone woman on a charitable mission. And yet there are people who cling to their dollars and dimes when her health is the stake. Mary Mays walks when she should be carried on the shoulders of grateful men."

At noon on November 29, 1916, friends of Mary Mays presented her with an automobile so she could better take care of the sick. Judge Frank J. Lahr, of the juvenile court, before a small group of friends on the east entrance to the court house, spoke of Mary's 20 years working for the Flower Mission. He thanked her for the assistance she had given to the Juvenile Court and other organizations. Representatives of the Flower Mission, the township trustee's office, the juvenile court and other institutions Mary had aided, were present.

The car paid dividends quickly. On December 5, 1916, Mary received a call to the home of 537 Concord Street, where Howard Wilson, age 21-months, was seriously ill. A doctor in the neighborhood told the mother the case was hopeless and the child would die.

After a quick examination, Mary drove the child to the city board of health for diphtheria antitoxin, a trip which made at a speed impossible before Mary received the automobile. Mary told *The News*, "I do not believe there is a happier woman in Indianapolis today, than Mrs. Wilson."

Occasionally, Mary Mays did speaking engagements. One such occasion was February 11, 1917. She and Judge Frank J.

Lahr of the Juvenile court, spoke to the "colored woman's branch" of the Y.W.C.A. at the Second Christian Church.

As a memorial to her late daughter Lucile, Mary presented an American flag to the community, to be raised July 30, 1917 at School No. 37 at 6 p.m. Mary also directed a fireworks display during the patriotic program. On October 8, 1917, Mary gave a talk to The Woman's Club on "First Aid Work."

MRS. MARY MAYS, NURSE TO
THE POOR, TO HAVE AUTOMOBILE

MRS. MARY MAYS.

Nurse Mary Mays making her rounds

On January 9, 1918, the Indianapolis
Flower Mission held its annual meeting and
appointed Mary E. Mays and Bessie Parry
as nurses. This would be the last year Mary
would serve with the Flower Mission.

Although in 1916 it was widely reported she had been there 21 years, her obituary stated she worked for the Flower Mission 25 years. She must have spent 7 years away from the Mission since she was appointed on an annual basis.

The Indianapolis Police Department was looking for 13 women to appoint as the first policewomen in the city's history. They wanted older women who had experience dealing with children and women, such as nurses, social workers and matrons. The choice of Mary Mays seemed a natural one.

On June 15, 1918, Mary Mays went to City Hall and received her police badge, number 7. She was then 5'6" tall and weighed 137 pounds. She and the other African-American woman appointed that day, Emma (Christy) Baker, also a native of Salem, Indiana, would be partners when they patrolled their beats – all "colored districts" in Indianapolis.

Mary Mays police photograph

After her appointment to the Indianapolis Police Department (at age 62), she and Emma Baker concentrated their duties on arresting shoplifters downtown, working as dance matrons, working with juveniles and protecting young women from predatory males. Another chief duty for policewomen in this era was as "Dance Matrons." Their job was to keep people from dancing too close or engaging in "immoral dancing."

One of the cases she worked on was on Oct. 17, 1918. A two-story home at 567 W. Merrill St. was full of 14 people, all seriously ill with pneumonia and influenza. These were members of the C.C. Owensby and Allen England families. Both families already had a baby who died. Emma England, age 35 and little Anna England, two months old, were critically ill.

This was during the great flu epidemic which killed millions. IPD dispatched two bicyclemen and Mays to deal with this situation. Two babies had already died.

The residents had not had any medical attention in two days and had no money. Mays and the male officers stayed at the home all night and cared for the needs of the family. Mays was relieved the next day by Policewoman Sadie Osborne.

Anna England died at 10 a.m. in City Hospital. Emma England died at the same instant, at another address she was had been taken to. Both died of pneumonia and influenza.

Sadie Osborne volunteered to take care of the victims until other aid could be found. She was relieved the afternoon of the 18th by two nurses from the American Red Cross.

Good news came to Mary Mays on March 14, 1919. She became a grandmother. Her daughter-in-law Harriett gave birth to a daughter named Mary J. Mays in Los Angeles, California.

On July 24, 1919, a mothers' meeting was held at the Y.M.C.A. recreational center. The address of the evening was delivered by "Mrs. Mary Mays, policewoman."

On August 17, 1920, three fires occurred in the home of Dr. Sumner A. Furnias, a City-Councilman. Police took in for questioning a 15-year old African-American girl living in his home on suspicion of arson. The job of questioning her was given to Officers Emma Baker and Mary Mays. Upon questioning, the girl told them that in addition to setting the fires, she put roach powder in their coffee and biscuits. The family became ill but didn't realize what the cause was until the girl confessed. She said she didn't think she was being treated properly.

Mary Mays personnel sheet.

Baker and Mays made a good record through 1921. On Jan. 3, 1922, a new administration took over the City of Indianapolis and many officers were asked to resign due to their political persuasion, which was the practice in those days. One of these was Mays. She and six other policewomen resigned on January 3rd. She left Indianapolis to live with her son Gerrold, in Los Angeles. She died there on June 1, 1928. Her burial place is unknown. She was living with her son Garrold E. Mays. Garrold died on July 22, 1960 at Riverside, California.

Mary Mays left a number of antiques to her nieces and nephews. She left wooden bandboxes with hats and bonnets from the 19th century in them and parasols with folding ivory handles for use in carriages.

She also left some sheepskin parchment "land grants" for land near Salem, Indiana. Mary also left an antique daybed which according to family lore, came from Virginia. She gave this to Mrs. Gertrude Crossen Hicks, a teacher in the Indianapolis public schools, her niece.

The daybed of Mary E. Mays.

Mary Jane Mays Browning[22]

---

[22] Photograph courtesy of Eric Browning

Mary Jane Mays, granddaughter of Mary (Roberts) Mays, who was born in 1919, married Warren K. Browning who she was married to 56 years.

"Janie" attended Los Angeles High School and started working as a switchboard operator after graduating. During WWII she was stationed at Fort Ord Army Base in Seaside, California, working for the American Legion.

She had resided in Davis, California since 1965. She was a member of the American Legion, the Davis PTA and was a Boy Scout mother.

Janie worked for the UC Davis at the Radiobiology Laboratory until retiring in 1984.

She was on the board of the Woodland Women's bowling Association for 26 years. She maintained a 145 average at the age of 86, when competing on the state senior circuit.

She died August 31, 2006. After a private
service in Monterey, California, her ashes
were scattered in Monterey Bay, near where
she had been stationed.

Clara (Hibbs) Crook was born April 17, 1874 at Three Rivers, St. Joseph County, Michigan, to Augustus and Adelaide (Weatherbee) Hibbs. In 1900, the family was living in Chicago, Clara working as a dress saleswoman.

She married September 11, 1901 to Thomas P. Crook in Chicago, who died in 1902. In

Chicago on June 25, 1904, Clara married Charles W. Habig of Indianapolis, Indiana. She was using the name Clara H. Crook when they married. Charles and Clara Habig resided at 3306 New Jersey Street in Indianapolis, 1910.

They had a son, Robert. Clara had volunteered several times as a social services worker at the Juvenile Court. Clara H. Crook was appointed June 15, 1918 as a policewoman with the Indianapolis Police Department. At the time she lived at 3233 Ruckle Street.

On July 2, 1918, Clara was given her first assignment, patrolling Riverside Park. Elizabeth Whiteman was her partner. As stated in Clara Burnside's biography, the pair made four arrests there within a week. Her shift was 1:30 p.m. to 11:30 p.m.

Apparently police work was not what Clara Crook wanted. She submitted her resignation to the Board of Safety on September 18, 1918. At some point Clara remarried to George M. Wagensler and settled in Birmingham, Alabama. Clara died December 5, 1937 and is buried in the Riverside Cemetery, Birmingham, Alabama.

Irene (Broughton) Beyer was born May 12, 1889 in Indianapolis, Indiana to Moses T. Broughton and Julia A. Widner. The family lived at 1002 Chadwick Street in 1900. Her

---

23 Official IPD portrait, 1921.

father was a salesman. Irene's mother died in 1903.

Irene married June 15, 1905 in Indianapolis, to Carl F. Beyer. Carl was a lieutenant with the Indianapolis Police Department and died on November 21, 1913 of typhoid fever.

Irene when she joined IPD, 1918.

When applications were taken for policewomen by the City of Indianapolis in 1918, Irene applied. The fact she was the widow of a firefighter weighed in her favor and she was appointed June 15, 1918. She was 5'7" and 170 pounds, so she could handle herself.

Irene was living at 602 North Alabama Street, 1920. On December 12, 1921, she was one of four policewomen selected by Inspector John Mullin to work for him in the IPD detective office. She began in that position on January 3, 1922. Her title was detective and her job was arresting unsuspecting shoplifters since she was in plain clothes.

One of these arrests occurred March 6, 1922 in a downtown store. A man named Ora Jones was reported to be taking articles from the counter. Policewomen Beyer and Bertha Duclus arrested him. Detective Beyer left to phone headquarters for the wagon.

When she did, the prisoner saw his chance and leaped over the nearest counter. Close behind was Bertha Duclus. She got a firm grip on Jones' belt and a coat lapel and the struggle was on. Duclus hung onto him until assistance came from Captain Michael Glenn. Jones was charged with petit larceny.

On May 5, 1922, detectives Duclus and Beyer were sitting on a bench in the waiting room at the Traction Terminal Station. A young woman sitting next to them began a conversation and it drifted to how she had trouble with a soldier at Ft. Harrison and she was on her way there to "get him."

She said, "Just to show you how tricky I am" as he pulled a revolver out of her waist." Duclus excused herself for a few minutes. When she returned, she and Irene Beyer asked the young woman to come outside to the curb.

"Just to show you how tricky we are, take a look at that", said the policewomen, pointing to a patrol wagon parked against the curb. The woman was arrested for carrying a concealed weapon.

When the IPD policewomen were allowed to buy a gun and took their first target practice on June 29, 1922, Irene proved herself a good shot, getting several bullseyes with her .32. Due to a manpower shortage, on September 27, 1922, Irene was transferred to the matron's office at the city prison.

On January 13, 1923 it was announced by the Mayor that Matron Irene Beyer would be placed in charge of four policewomen to be assigned to the newly created Housing and Sanitation Division.

This was probably a short assignment because the chief of police Herman Rikhoff was upset when he heard about it. Irene was transferred to the office of the city controller, where she was working in 1924.

Irene Beyer noticed a group of five boys aged 8 to 13, trying to steer a large car, on June 17, 1926. She stopped the auto and found out it was stolen earlier in the day from 13th and Missouri Streets. She requested assistance and a motor policeman came and the boys were taken to the detention home.

In this era, it was common for police officers to take up a collection for someone who was down and out. This happened to Irene Beyer and fellow policewoman Mary Moriarty, September 6, 1926. They saw a 19-year old girl who was on her way home to Church, Kentucky in the Union Station. She had no money. The officers collected money to buy her a train ticket.

Irene was one of 15 policewomen who were due to lose their jobs, due to no money being in the city's 1927 budget. She kept her job after a lawsuit brought an injunction against the city. Irene was working as a clerk in the accident prevention bureau at police headquarters when she was overcome by 90-degree temperature on July 19, 1928. She was taken to her house by a city hospital ambulance with heat prostration.

She was one of the policewomen downgraded to the new rank of Fifth Grade Patrolman on October 18, 1932. The Board of Safety promoted her to Fourth Class policewoman on December 26, 1933, a late Christmas present.

Irene Beyer personnel sheet.

Irene was working on the telephone switchboard in police headquarters in 1933 to 1934. Irene Beyer retired in 1939. She had served in the city controller's office, the detective department, the accident prevention office and as a city park matron.

When she retired, she moved to Martinsville, where her family originated. She died there, October 11, 1942. Irene was buried in Crown Hill Cemetery.

Ella Teresa (Dugan) Gregoire was born April 17, 1858 in Indianapolis, Indiana to Thomas and Mary Dugan, Irish immigrants. The family was living at 304 South Pennsylvania Street, June 14, 1880. Ella is listed in the June 12, 1880 census of Indianapolis, Indiana as a live-in servant of John Bevan, a grocer at 90 West 1st Street. She later married Louis Gregoire, who died March 8, 1886.

Ella was appointed 1894 as Matron in the Marion County Workhouse. She was appointed December 22, 1897 as Matron for the Indianapolis Police Department. She had to determine her own job duties since there was no one there to tell her.

The job consisted of interviewing new female inmates and counseling them. She was an intermediary between inmates and the judge and prosecutor if they were a first offender.

When she was first hired, the male members of the Indianapolis Police Department looked upon a matron as an experiment. The following article describes her hiring:

"Two police matrons, at $50 a month each were hired for the new police building. The appointees are: Mrs. Ella Gregoire and Miss Rena Reisner, matrons. Mrs. Gregoire assumes her new duties, Dec. 27th as the resignation of Mrs. Anna Buchanan, the present matron, reads to take effect Jan. 1 Buchanan leaves to be married. Mrs.

Gregoire is a widow, 36 years of age, residing at 2153 N. Pennsylvania St. She has acted as assistant matron at the county workhouse, and also as a nurse. She was born in Indianapolis and has lived here most of her life. She was highly recommended for the position.

Miss Reisner is about 40 years of age and has had experience in dealing with young people in private families. She has had no public experience. The mayor says she was highly recommended for the position, but she had no application on file in the safety board's office."

The Indianapolis Sun, December 22, 1897.

The following was published in the
Indianapolis Journal in 1904 about Ella
Gregoire.

MATRON ELLA GREGOIRE.

MATRON ELLA GREGOIRE.

The matrons at the police station form peculiar friendships with some of the prisoners and as a result are very accustomed to having Belle or Kitty, or May, or some other well-known character pay the calls at all times of the day and night. Oftentimes, however, they come to the police station from a matter of choice.

One morning several months ago, Matron Ella Gregoire was sitting in her office reading a newspaper when in stepped May Kauffman, a police character, who had been arrested times innumerable.

The woman had evidently been drinking, but she said: "Mrs. Gregoire, I just came down to market and bought this chicken for the people I am working for and I thought I would run up and tell you how well I am getting along. I've reformed, too." she exclaimed enthusiastically. During the conversation that followed, the kind-hearted matron advised her "friend" to be careful when she got on the street and go right home or she would get drunk and be back at the police station. The woman went away and when the noon hour *came, the matron turned her keys over to the turnkey while she went to lunch.*

When she returned and opened the door, lying on the table was a half-picked chicken and two loaves of bread that had evidently been rolled about the street. The explanation was soon found. May had left the matron's office, got drunk, fallen on the chicken, killed it and tried to pick it on the street. She was busily engaged in that practice when the bicyclemen were called to arrest her.

Mrs. Gregoire has had many other laughable experiences with the unfortunate women that are daily placed in the cells, yet she has always been so kind-hearted that she is loved by the most vile women brought there. Recently a woman left in the station house and sent to the jail crocheted a table centerpiece for her while she whiled away her hours in jail.

Mrs. Gregoire was born in Indianapolis in 1856. Her maiden name was Dugan and she was married to Louis Gregoire. Fourteen years ago her husband died and she was left with a family to support. For two years she served as matron at the workhouse, for eight years served as a private nurse and has been at the police station since that.

Ella Gregoire and Rena Reisner had both worked as matrons at police headquarters since 1897. They worked 12-hour shifts, one coming in at 7 a.m. and staying until 6 p.m., the other replacing her. There would have been few if any days off. This is why their predecessor resigned after working 6 years without a day off.

Mrs. Gregoire answered this way when asked if the job was a strain on her mind and body, in an April 1904 interview: "You see, I do not live here inside of the station house. My home is outside and when I leave this place I never think of it again until it is time to again come on duty…when I first began this work I thought about it continually, and whenever a prisoner was sentenced I suffered as much as she did, and when she was discharged by the judge I rejoiced with her also, but I saw this would never do, for I was continually on a nervous strain."

Continuing, she said, "When court convenes every morning the matron has to go and look after her prisoners. After her cases have been disposed of she brings her prisoners back, and those that go to the workhouse have to be escorted to the wagon; others who have jail sentences she has to see are sent to the jail." Matron Gregoire described having to care for women who were insane, which was depressing to her.

Matron Ella Gregoire at her desk, February 1914.

After being appointed a policewoman in 1918, Gregoire was told to report back to her old job, as Matron in the city prison, effective July 2nd.

1914 photograph of the women's cells in the "prison" on the 2nd floor of the Indianapolis Police Department headquarters, where the matrons worked.

With the arrival of the new mayor in 1922, Matron Gregoire was ordered to retire or resign. She retired on January 2, 1922 and moved to Cleveland Heights, Ohio, where she was living in 1930. She then moved to Miami, Florida. She died in 1948, Polk

---

[24] Official IPD portrait, 1921.

County, Florida. She is buried in Oak Hill
Burial Park, Lakeland, Florida.

Ella Gregoire Personnel Sheet

Elizabeth (Whiteman) Gillespie was born about 1874. Her father was born in Virginia, mother in Pennsylvania.

She began working as a matron at the Marion County Jail and then accepted a position on August 7, 1902 as assistant matron at the Indiana Women's Prison. She did this because the assistant matron was ill. On August 14th the woman recovered and took her job back, Elizabeth being out of a job suddenly. Fortunately, she got her old job back at the County Jail. Elizabeth became a matron for the city prison on April 16, 1910.

On November 14, 1911, Elizabeth Whiteman and Rena Reisner, matrons at IPD, both declined positions as detectives on the city police force, offered by Mayor Lew Shank. Both told the mayor and Superintendent of Police Martin Hyland that they were well satisfied with their present employment and were not seeking other positions.

Each Christmas, Matron Whiteman was given a Christmas present by the court. She would get to select an inmate and the judge would release her. On December 24, 1913, Josie Myers appeared before Judge Collins, charged with intoxication. Elizabeth Whiteman stepped forward but was stopped by the judge, who said "Your

Christmas gift, Miss Whiteman" and stamped the affidavit as "judgement withheld."   Josie Myers went home for Christmas.

In May 1916, the International Policewomen's Association held their annual conference in Indianapolis. Attending were IPD Matrons Elizabeth Whiteman, Annie Buchanan Logan and Ella Gregoire. Also there was Mrs. Alice Stebbins Wells, first policewoman in U.S. history, of the Los Angeles Police Department.

Elizabeth Whiteman was highly qualified when the Indianapolis Board of Safety was seeking applicants for the position of policewoman in 1918 and this time, she took the job. When appointed to IPD, she was badge number 10. She received badge number 155 three months later.

Her first assignment on July 2, 1918 was to patrol Riverside Park, from 1:30 p.m. to 11:30 p.m. She and partner Irene Beyer investigated 41 complaints in the month of October 1918.

Elizabeth secretly married IPD Traffic
Officer Samuel Gillespie on December 17,
1919 in Chicago, Illinois. In 1920 the couple
lived at 234 North Mount Street.

Elizabeth Gillespie personnel sheet.

On August 31, 1920, Elizabeth handed in
her resignation to Clara Burnside, her
supervisor and asked that it be effective
that day. Samuel and Elizabeth Gillespie
were returning to Indianapolis in 1940 from
a car trip to California. While stopping in

El Paso, Texas, she passed away on January 21st. She is buried in Crown Hill Cemetery.

Sarena "Rena" Reisner was born October 30, 1856 Newton, Jasper County, Illinois to Christian Reisner and Margaret Brooks. Her father was a native of Darmstadt, Hessen, Germany.

Christian Reisner and his family farmed $5,000 worth of land near Newton, Illinois in 1870. Sarena, aged 13, was one of 9 children in the home. They were still there in 1880 and Sarena was now 23, living at home. By 1886, "Rena" Reisner had relocated to Indianapolis, Indiana and was living at 241 North Tennessee. In 1896 she was working as a dressmaker.

Rena was appointed December 22, 1897 as Matron for the Indianapolis Police Department. She and Ella Gregoire, also hired that day as a matron, were the second female employees in the history of the Indianapolis Police Department. For some reason however, Rena didn't start until March 10, 1898.

In 1900, Rena Reisner was living in Indianapolis, at 429 North Capitol Avenue with her two adult cousins. Rena was a caring individual. One example came in May 1904. One of the inmates "Louise" was a chronic drunk. The mother in Illinois was thinking she had a good job in Indianapolis and wrote Rena saying Louise would be welcome home whenever she got tired of "working." Rena was trying to get Louise back in shape to return home to her loving mother, without her disgrace being known.

LIKES TO SHOOT GUN:
SHE IS POLICE MATRON

-GEO-BREHM-

MATRON RENA REISNER.

Police Matron Rena Reisner is fond of shooting of shooting a real gun.

And she does not hunger for target shooting, either. She pines for a trip, these snowy days to the home of her brother in Illinois, with whom she has many a time shouldered a gun and marched through woodland and pasture land in pursuit of the elusive rabbit.

Women who like to fire a rifle are easy to find, but Miss Reisner, with her desire for a few hours in the snow with a real booming, "kicking" shotgun probably has little company among the women of Indiana.

On November 14, 1911, Elizabeth Whiteman and Rena Reisner, matrons at IPD, both declined positions as detectives on the city police force, offered by Mayor Lew Shank. Both told the mayor and Superintendent of Police Martin Hyland that they were well satisfied with their present employment and were not seeking other positions.

"I thought Mrs. Reisner would make a first-class detective," said the mayor, 'because she put up a warm fight with a man who attempted to steal her purse. Her reputation already is established, and I believe she and Matron Whiteman could fill the positions very acceptably.

Like her co-workers Elizabeth Whiteman and Ella Gregoire, long-time matrons, all three were appointed the first policewomen in Indianapolis history, June 15, 1918.

For her first assignment on July 2, 1918, Rena was sent to patrol Union Station and the Traction Terminal Station from 1:30 p.m. to 11:30 p.m. She did this and other police duties for 16 months, and then returned to her job as a matron in the city prison.

Rena Reisner - 1921

The new Mayor, Lew Shank ordered Rena and the other two former matrons to retire or quit on January 2, 1922.

Rena Reisner Personnel sheet

While the other two retired, on January 4, 1922, Rena was ordered back to work by the Board of Safety.   She did retire three months later, however, April 1, 1922. She was 66 years old.

Rena's desire after 24 years of caring for unfortunate women was to raise chickens on a farm in Zionsville, a little town northwest of Indianapolis.

Recalling her early days when she retired, Rena said, "The women prisoners of the old days were a much rougher lot than the ones of the last ten years." She said the matrons had to fight about every time the police sent in a prisoner then. She still carried a scar on her right forearm as a remembrance from one of those "battles."

She was about to search a woman "dope fiend" when the prisoner attacked her and bit a piece out of her arm. Blood poisoning developed and for a time the doctors thought she might lose the arm.

Rena Reisner died on June 13, 1930 near Zionsville, Indiana of diabetes. She was buried in Crown Hill Cemetery.

Hethe Helen Johnson, known as "Hettie", was born March 7, 1875 in Bowling Green, Kentucky to Major and Anna (Jones) Johnson. They lived in Terre Haute, Indiana, 1880-93. She married John Reeves and had two daughters by him. In 1898 Hettie was living in Paris, Illinois.

She came to Indianapolis from Danville, Illinois in 1898. She married June 15, 1908 to Robert L. Brewer. Hettie was a member of the Second Baptist Church, directing the Jewel Band for children there in 1909.

Eight women met on February 23, 1912 and organized a club to be known as the Time and Tide club. Hettie was elected treasurer. Later that year, they renamed it the West End Utility Club.

The West End Utility Club elected Hettie Brewer its vice-president in September 1912. Hettie then lived at 417 West St. Clair Street. This would be the club's place to meet in the future. She became club president in February 1913.

Three days after the Great Flood of 1913 struck the west side of Indianapolis, a mass meeting was held at Bethel A.M.E. Church March 30th. African-American citizens gathered to aid in the relief work for people affected by the flood. Hettie Brewer was selected to be a co-director of the effort.

Hettie was chosen by the West End Utility Club in July 1914 to be a representative at the National Association of Colored Women's Clubs (NACWC) convention at

Wilberforce, Ohio in August 1914. She became quite ill at home in August.

"Colored Women's Day" was observed on December 6, 1914, under the auspices of the NACWC. This social organization raised money for WWI, worthy causes and also raised awareness of the lynching problem in America. Hettie was chairman of the committee on arrangements for the event, which had featured speakers and a musical program.

At the January 15, 1915 West End Utility Club's annual reception, Hettie gave the address of welcome to the 60 members in attendance and reviewed the year's work. She entertained the members of the NACWC on January 18, 1915 also.

She was chosen by the West End Utility Club as a delegate to the State federation, to be held in May, 1915.

She was a delegate to the NACWC meeting held in Anderson Indiana in June 1916.

Hettie was a skilled baker and operated Brewer's Café from 1915 to 1916 at 422 Indiana Avenue.

Brewer's Cafe, 422 Indiana Ave

with quidk service, visit Brewres
Cafe 442 Indiana avenue.   Prsvate din
-ing room also.

Sunday Menu.

Chicken broth with rice.
Chicken Pot pie.
Roast Beef with brown gravy.
Roast Pork with apple sauce.
Candied sweet potatoes.
Snow flake Irish potatoes.
English Peas.
Spagetti; Combination salad
Cream and peaches – Cake.
Coffee, tea butter and sweetmilk.
Mrs. Hettie Brewer, Proprietor.
H. W. Lourton, Manager

The Indianapolis Recorder – February 13, 1915

During that same period, she was president of the West End Utility Club, a woman's group. For the year 1916-1917, Hettie Brewer served as chairperson of the committee on religion for the State NACWC. Hettie opened a restaurant in her home at 417 West St. Clair Street in December 1916.

She applied with the Indianapolis Police Department and was appointed January 2, 1922, replacing Mary Mays, who resigned that same day. Hettie was 5'5", 143 pounds.

She was patrolling the African-American districts by August of that year. She was one of the three policewomen sent from one city agency to another in early 1923. On January 13, 1923, Hettie Brewer was assigned to a newly created division of Housing & Sanitation, assigned to inspect sanitary conditions, along with 4 other policewomen. Previously she had been assigned to the traffic division, as a "meter maid".

On February 22, 1923 she was assigned to collect fines in the Clerk's Office of the City Court. She and Anna Buck had collected several hundred dollars and had made a number of arrests by March.

On March 8, 1923, Policewoman Brewer was sent out from the Clerk's Office with commitment papers for the re-arrest of Ernest Cosby, age 17, of 1324 Yandes Street. Policewoman Emma Baker of the Juvenile Court joined her.

Hattie and Emma found Cosby at home and placed him under arrest. He pretended to get his cap, and then bolted out the door. Hattie made a flying tackle, grabbing his overcoat but he slipped out and ran down Yandes Street, "at forty miles an hour" as described by the women.

Brewer and Baker gave chase, Hettie firing three times at Cosby as was permitted in 1923, but this only served to make him run faster. As they approached the Big Four railroad tracks, in a scene the newspaper described as being a "slapstick movie chase", the policewomen were gaining on the suspect, but he jumped across the railroad track just as a freight train cut across their path, halting the chase.

Early the next day, Policewomen Brewer and Baker returned to Cosby's home, found

him in bed and brought him to police
headquarters – without his cap.

1924 – Left to right:
Emma Baker & Hettie Baker.

Hettie was found to be absent from her district on Indiana Avenue, the evening of December 7, 1923. Lt. Anderson and Sergeant Ball found her eating dinner at home, 417 East St. Clair Street. She said she had been taking an hour break for dinner during her 8-hour shift.

Taken to police headquarters, Captain Edward Schubert ordered Hettie to surrender her badge but she refused to do so, trying to explain the circumstances. She finally handed it in.

Hettie Brewer was charged December 11, 1923 with neglect of duty & absence without leave and suspended retroactively to December 7, 1923 by Chief Rikhoff. Hettie was tried before the Board of Safety on December 18, 1923. Her case was taken under advisement until December 26, 1923.

On December 26th, the board found her not guilty of absence without leave. She was found guilty of neglect of duty. They docked her pay from December 7th to 25th while she was suspended. She was ordered to report to duty December 26th at 3 p.m.

Hettie Brewer personnel card

Each night in the spring of 1924, Hettie visited dance halls frequented by African-Americans, to perform Dance Matron duties. She was assisted on Saturday nights by Policewoman Emma Baker.

A man named Ross Majors, 46, was arrested September 7, 1926 by Treasury Officers Holmes and Sturgeon, who stated they purchased a small amount of "white mule" whiskey from Majors. He was operating a stand at the State Fair Grounds.

Chief Claude F. Johnson

Chief Claude F. Johnson began an investigation after he received information that Majors and Hettie Brewer were operating the stand, known as a "Blind

---

[25] IMPD Lichtenberger History Room.

Tiger" as partners. She was alleged to have "staked" Majors. During Prohibition, this was illegal. Hettie was on vacation when the arrest occurred. Hettie resigned by phone on September 8th and turned in her resignation September 14, 1926, effective retroactively to September 8th.

Hettie put on a play, December 30, 1926 at Barnes Methodist Episcopal Chapel under the auspices of the Aid Society.

On June 22, 1927, Hettie remarried to Thomas H. Vaulx.

Hettie suffered from a chronic illness the last five years of her life. She fell at home on July 29, 1943, breaking her left leg badly. She died on August 9th at City Hospital. She then lived at 2816 Boulevard Place. She lived to see six African-American policewomen appointed that same year, the first since she was appointed.

At death, she was described as a well-known and highly respected citizen of Indianapolis who was a religious, social and political worker. She was survived by two daughters, Anna (Reeves) Kennerly and

Eula (Reeves) House. She is buried in Crown Hill Cemetery, Indianapolis, Indiana.

Morrissey's Purge

Chief Michael Morrissey

Michael F. Morrissey became chief of the Indianapolis Police Department on June 16, 1931. At age 32, he was one of the youngest chiefs in department history. He is known for being one of the most innovative men to ever hold that rank in IPD history.

However, he did not like the idea of women being police officers. On July 8, 1931, he moved two policewomen who were working behind a desk at headquarters to a downtown walking beat.

Mary Moore, in the Accident Prevention Bureau and Anna Brunner, who was in the Traffic Department were moved to a beat which was bounded from Capitol Avenue to East Street and from Union Station to St. Clair Street, working from 4 p.m. to midnight. This comprised most of what is now known as "the mile square", or most of downtown Indianapolis.

They joined three other policewomen already moved onto that beat. Chief Morrissey said this was done in the interests of greater efficiency.

Mayor Reginald H. Sullivan

Reginald H. Sullivan became Mayor of Indianapolis in 1930. He wasn't subtle about his plans for the 18 policewomen who worked for him. On December 29, 1931, he stated that definite plans for terminating their positions, which have been branded as "useless", have not been completed.

The Board of Safety still promoted four of the policewomen this same date to the rank of matron, a higher paying position. They were Anna Peats, Mary Cantlon, Lillian Jaschka and Nell Dunkle.

Chief Michael Morrissey said the plans to discharge the policewomen was "news to me" but would be welcome news if it happened.

It was hinted that technical charges may be filed with the Board of Safety in their effort to replace the women with male officers. Several policewomen said they would take court action to retain their jobs.

Two policewomen were suspended on July 16, 1932 for failure to obey orders, according to Chief Michael F. Morrissey. They were Elizabeth Denny, assigned to Garfield Park and Margaret Hildebrand, assigned to Ellenberger Park. Both women said they were absent from duty but had reported to the main office through pay telephones instead of the police Gamewell system.

Margaret Hildebrand said she had gone to a shop a few blocks away to have her badge repaired so that she could wear it. While engaged in this, Lieutenant Frank Owen, head of the IPD accident prevention bureau came looking for her and reported her absent without leave.

Elizabeth Denny said she waited at a Gamewell call box for over 30 minutes after she was due to make a regular call to headquarters to report. Lieutenant Owen also filed charges against her.

Chief Morrissey by now had said several times he would try and eliminate the policewomen from the department. The *Indianapolis Star* noted that these had been tried several times previously but that each time the women were victorious in court. This time, Hildebrand and Denny had attorney Ira M. Holmes for their trial before the Board of Safety on August 16th.

The Board of Safety took their cases under advisement after hearing testimony that day. The *Indianapolis Star* stated the next day that the trials of the two women were regarded as the first step to remove policewomen from the force.

Meanwhile, other policewomen had been removed from clerical positions and assigned to walk a beat in districts which formerly belonged to male officers. The worst incident that had occurred to date involving an Indianapolis policewoman happened on July 22, 1932.

Policewoman Mary Moore, in stopping a man from viciously beating a youth in Sullivan Park, had the suspect turn on her. She showed her badge and pulled her gun on the man, telling him he was under arrest. He lunged at her, taking her gun and throwing Officer Moore to the ground.

The Indianapolis Star, in its report of this incident, praised Officer Moore for sticking to her post and said the decision of Chief Michael Morrissey to assign policewomen from clerical jobs to men's districts was an effort to induce them to resign. Under state law they cannot be discharged except for disciplinary cause.

All of the policewomen reported to their walking beats, despite being assigned to undesirable districts, which are known to police as "tough spots." Policewoman

Moore, the Star said, "drew the toughest, perhaps because her husband also is a member of the police department."

A male veteran policeman, Alfred Ray, was attacked and beaten and stoned severely at Sullivan Park on August 29, 1922. Sullivan Park was the meeting place for the Ford and Carey gangs. Other gangs were still present in the park, along with "radicals", vagrants and gamblers.

On August 30th, the Board of Safety fired both policewomen on recommendation from Chief Morrissey. The charge was neglect of duty. This left 16 policewomen on the Indianapolis Police Department in 1932.

When asked how many policewomen were now left on the force, Chief Michael Morrissey replied, "Too many."

Lieutenant Ralph Dean

Policewoman Mary Moore was the next
policewoman to face the wrath of Chief
Morrissey. She was suspended September
3, 1932. Lieutenant Ralph Dean reported
that Officer Moore had been "riding around
in an automobile on her district", which was

in violation of departmental regulation. She refused to obey orders when he ordered her into an automobile to take her from 34th and Illinois Streets, where he saw her, to police headquarters.

Mary Moore stated that Lieutenant Dean had been watching her and when she stepped up to an automobile, in which her husband, Edward Moore, an IPD officer, had just brought her lunch money, Dean demanded to know how she had been spending her time.

On September 4th, Mary Moore turned in her badge and resigned, rather than going through a trial before the Board of Safety.

Moore said she refused to ride with Lieutenant Dean to headquarters, being driven instead by her husband. She also denied having been in the automobile or being lax in her duties.

Policewomen had been assigned on September 1st to men's districts when the city parks were closed for the season. Moore was assigned to district No. 29, which ran from 30th Street north to the city limits, and from Northwestern Avenue east to Illinois Street, from 7 a.m. to 7 p.m. She was the only police officer assigned to that district.

Mary Moore said she had a premonition that she would "be next to go" after the terminations of Policewomen Denny and Hildebrand. It was known that Morrissey said since he was prevented legally from discharging them, he intended to eliminate them one by one as the occasion offered.

On the evening of September 12, 1932 at a meeting of the Indianapolis Federation of Civic Community Clubs, a resolution was adopted that their opinion was that policewomen should be retained.

While they voted, Chief Morrissey suspended Policewoman Margaret V. Osborne, the 4th that month. He charged that she failed to report a minor traffic accident in writing.

Another indignity suffered by the policewomen came on October 18, 1932. A recent ordinance created by the city council created the ranks of third, fourth and fifth grade patrolmen. On this day, fifteen of the policewomen were assigned to these new, lower paying ranks and received pay cuts. Bertha was moved to a Fourth class designation, earning less than $1,300 annually. Since they were first appointed in 1918, policewomen earned the same salary as their male counterparts.

The other policewomen were given these ranks:

Fifth Grade - $1,000 Annual Salary

Emma Baker
Irene Beyer
Anna Brunner
Metta Davis
Leona Frankfort
Lourena Fullilove
Mary Moriarty
Margaret Osborne

Fourth Grade – Less than $1,300 Annual Salary

Bertha Duclus
Ruth Haywood
Cozette Osborn

Third Grade - $1,500 Annual Salary – All Police Matrons

Mary Cantlon
Nell Dunkle
Anna Peats
Lillian Jaschka

Margaret B. Self was born February 24, 1874 in Indianapolis, Indiana to Barry and Sarah (Grooms) Self. Margaret had three years of Business College after graduating from high school.

She married Harry F. Hildebrand on February 10, 1891 in Indianapolis, Indiana. They were married at the Self family home. They left for a honeymoon in the south. The couple lived with her parents at 719 North New Jersey Street, 1900. Harry Hildebrand was then a constable.

The Hildebrand's had these children: Marie Caroline, born February 10, 1892, Helen T., Marjorie A. and Harold S. Hildebrand.

Harry Hildebrand owned his own detective agency in 1910. The couple lived at 608 North New Jersey Street then. They later lived at 1824 North Alabama Street. She was a member of the Central Christian Church.

Margaret became the first female Constable in Marion County, Indiana history, June 16, 1917. The board of county commissioners decided to appoint her constable for Warren Township. She was assigned to the court of Justice of the Peace White.

She was constable when appointed to the Indianapolis Police Department on October 21, 1919 as a policewoman. She was issued badge number 281. Margaret was 5'8", 152 pounds.

Margaret resigned on January 2, 1922 from IPD when the new administration came in, as did other policewomen. However, she was reappointed a policewoman on May 10, 1922.

When the city tried to lay her off in 1926, she was one of the four policewomen who filed a lawsuit, which brought an injunction that stopped the action.

Margaret Hildebrand in 1921.

Margaret Hildebrand personnel sheet.

On August 30, 1932, the Board of Public Safety dismissed Officer Margaret Hildebrand in a move to force policewomen from the force, according to the Indianapolis newspapers. She was fired for neglect of duty for leaving her post. She filed suit September 10, 1932, saying the board was prejudiced against her because she was a woman. She said she left Ellenberger Park to get her badge repaired.

Margaret died on May 2, 1941 in
Indianapolis.   She is buried in Crown Hill
Cemetery.

Mary T. Kelly was born January 12, 1868 in Indianapolis, Indiana to Cornelius Kelly and Margaret Kennedy, Irish immigrants. Cornelius Kelly was born near Cahirciveen, County Kerry, Ireland. He came to Indianapolis in 1859.

---

[26] Official IPD portrait.

Cornelius Kelly resided at 474 West New York Street and for many years was a coach painter. He was a candidate once for Recorder on the Democratic Party ticket and had a wide acquaintance.

Mary Kelly wed Thomas E. Cantlon on November 30, 1893 in Indianapolis. By 1900, Thomas Cantlon was deceased and Mary was living with her parents. She had a three-year-old daughter, Margaret.

Mary was working as a stenographer for the Judges of the State Supreme Court, 1907. She was a clerk for the court, 1910. In 1912 she was a Notary Public. She worked later as a probation officer.

Mary Cantlon was appointed to the Indianapolis Police Department on October 21, 1919. In 1921, she was assigned as a Matron in the jail.

An unusual event in local police history occurred on August 29, 1928. A Charles H. Krause, 66, was giving a speech on the corner of Market and Illinois Streets to a gathering crowd. This was a common scene, as has stood on a dry goods box to share his thoughts on religion nine times, usually taken home by police or to jail, the last time, when he called the American flag, "the grand old rag."

Krause changed himself to a post and threw the key away in a gesture of triumph. The key hit a man named George Craig on the cheek, as he said the police would not take him from that spot.

Craig found the key on the ground. As he was looking at it, Policewoman Mary Cantlon saw Krause's actions and called police headquarters and asked that a squad and a hacksaw be sent immediately to the location. She had summoned officers to get Mr. Krause before.

Mr. Craig recognized Mary Cantlon and told her he had the key. She called headquarters and countermanded her order for the hacksaw but not for the squad.

Mr. Krause was now being heckled and things were becoming heated. The squad still hadn't arrived so she hailed a passing IPD squad car with Sergeant Michael Morrissey (future Chief) and Patrolmen Henry Ludgin and William Ennis. She gave them the key.

"Here they come!" yelled the crowd. The burley men in blue pushed through to Krause. The padlock was taken off and Krause shoved in the police car. Chief Claude Worley ordered him taken home.

Mary's beat in 1926 included patrolling the Traction Terminal Station.

Mary Cantlon on March 1, 1927 declared a burlesque show "Bright Eyes", "rank and vulgar", which was closed down.

She received a promotion to Matron on December 29, 1931. She was promoted to Patrolman Third Class in 1937. She continued as a Matron through August 5, 1939, when she retired from IPD.

For the last two years of her career, she was credited with the social rehabilitation of many prisoners coming under her care. She retired the same day as Policewoman Emma Baker.

Mary died May 11, 1944 of a stroke at her Indianapolis home. She was buried in Holy Cross Cemetery.

²⁷

Mae M. Rupert was born July 31, 1890 in Indiana to Charles and Hortensia Rupert. The family lived at 2498 Orchard Avenue in 1900. The father was a house painter.

---

27 Official IPD portrait from 1920.

In 1920, Mae Rupert resided with her Aunt Stella Park at 831 North Pine Street. Mae was working as a cashier in a grocery store then. That year, she applied for and was appointed a policewoman with the Indianapolis Police Department, on September 7th. She was issued badge number 54. She was then 5'7", 148 pounds.

When the Shank administration took office on January 2, 1922, the Board of Safety requested her resignation, but reappointed her on March 1, 1922, receiving badge number 78 this time.

March 1, 1922.

Hon. Board of Public Safety,
City of Indianapolis.

Gentlemen:-   Mae M. Rupert - Police Force.

I have not had time to go out on this application but John Mullin, Supervisor of Detectives, recommends this woman very highly for reinstatement. He says that he knows her personally and her record as Policewoman is excellent and requests that she be reinstated.

Respectfully,

Saml Gadshi

She took a position in the detective division under Inspector John Mullen after taking the oath on March 8th. She was assigned to undercover shoplifting prevention duties.

A man named Hence Orme, a well-known farmer, was fatally wounded on November 16, 1922. A Miss Nell McCune was interviewed by IPD Detectives Golder and Sullivan. Female detectives Sarah Rogers and Mae Rupert remained in the room while McCune gave her answers.

On June 17, 1924, Mae was ordered to be examined by the Police Surgeon. On the basis of this, she was granted 6-months of leave effective that date and received another 6-months of leave on December 16, 1924, evidently due to a serious illness.

Mae resigned from IPD on April 27, 1926. She was one of 140 officers to leave the force that year.

Mae Rupert personnel sheet.

In May of 1929, Mae sold a grocery store that she owned. She was working as a stenographer for the Internal Revenue in 1930.

Mae was sworn in as Marion County Deputy Sheriff, on February 14, 1931, to serve as dance hall matron, along with 7 other women.

Mae Rupert and her sister Anna Faulkenberg resided at 3055 North Illinois Street in 1955. She had worked as an agent for Jewel Companies, Inc. She was a member of the Glendale Seventh-day Adventist Church of Indianapolis.

She died on November 21, 1973, in Evansville, Indiana. She is buried in Crown Hill Cemetery.

Metta B. Davis was born in April 1870, in Hickman, Fulton County, Kentucky to Eliza Davis. She was living with her sister Katherine Deitch, 431 East Pratt Street, Indianapolis, Indiana in 1900. Metta was a member of the Consumers' League. In 1915, one of their potential issues was that of policewomen in Indianapolis.

Metta spent several months in Hot Springs, Arkansas, returning to Indianapolis in April, 1917. Her brother Captain John H. Davis lived in Pendleton, Arkansas.

Metta was a supervisor at the Nordyke & Marmon Aviation Factory, 1918-20. In 1920, she was still living with her sister. Metta was 49 and single.

Metta was appointed to the Indianapolis Police Department on September 21, 1920. She was issued badge number 20. Metta was 5'7", 152 pounds. Her 90-day probation period ended September 28th, along with that of Nell Dunkle, Mae Rupert and Margaret Osborn. With the addition of these four policewomen, Indianapolis was set to surpass Washington D.C. as having the most female police officers in the world.

Mayor Lew Shank announced on December 23, 1921 that Captain Clara Burnside would be assigned to the Juvenile Court as a Sergeant and among her female investigators would be Miss Metta Davis.

While in juvenile court, Metta Davis and Margaret Hildebrand found four children ranging in age from three months to five years, at a boarding house for babies. One child was returned to its mother and the policewomen worked on March 22, 1923 at finding the parents of the other three.

"Raiding" the boarding house, the policewomen found only one bed in the part of the house where the children were kept. The five-year-old was doing housework and taking care of some of the other children. The children were half-starved. The babies were dirty and poorly fed and clothed.

The policewomen found one child's parent and returned the child to her. Based on the report of the policewomen, charges would be filed against the woman keeping the boarding house, where the conditions were "deplorable."

In March of 1924, Metta and Anna Brunner worked on Saturday nights as a Dance Matron.

Metta Davis investigated another case of child abuse on September 20, 1924. At 331 Koehne Street, after a woman fled an abusive husband, five young boys were left deserted. A sixth was a handicapped and fighting for his life after being carried from the home by the mother.

The father refused to feed the children. Metta testified at a hearing in Marion County Juvenile Court that she found several empty whiskey bottles when she went into the house. What little furniture was in it was overturned and there was evidence of a struggle.

Metta was one of the policewomen who sued the city in 1926 when they attempted to eliminate their jobs.

Metta was living at 514 East 34th Street in 1932 when she appeared in Juvenile court on August 5th. While there, someone stole her purse, which contained her badge and $25. "Imagine my embarrassment!" she said.

The suspect, later apprehended, was a man with a mental disorder. He appeared in court December 4, 1932. He was given a one-to-ten-year sentence for grand larceny but the sentence was suspended.

On November 20, 1934, Investigator Metta Davis was checking into an anonymous letter which led her to 1302 West Market Street. A 16-year old girl was allegedly being held against her will there.

Metta used a skeleton key to gain admittance to the home. She called out Patrolmen John Moriarty and Elmer Cleary from headquarters when she couldn't gain entrance to a room which the girl was in. Entrance was forced and Helen Mack, 16 years of age and weighing only 70 pounds, was found. Metta said she found Helen huddled in the room, its doors and window locked, dark and unventilated.

She told a story of being held prisoner there for two years and being fed two daily servings of "potatoes and gravy." The father, Harry Mack and stepmother, Ora Mack, were arrested at other locations for child neglect. The father claimed they kept her prisoner because she was always trying to steal things and they were afraid she was a kleptomaniac.

She clutched two apples given her by Metta Davis and another policewoman as she was assisted to a car, too weak to walk. She was taken to the juvenile home, where she was bathed and well fed. She said she never wanted to see her parents again.

In 1938, Metta was assigned as a Matron in the city jail. On July 27, 1941, Metta was walking on 11th Street near Superior Street late at night when a boy ran up behind her and grabbed her purse. It contained her badge, service revolver and several police cards.

Metta was assigned to the new Juvenile Aid Division where in August 1941 she went to a new headquarters located at 19-21 South Alabama Street.

Metta and Policewoman Lourena Fullilove investigated a case of child abuse in January 1946. Two sisters, Lorraine and Barbara Hankins, aged 5 and 6, had been whipped with a leather strap and sometimes tied in a cow stall in the barn by two people who had custody of them.

The policewomen filed charges against the custodians of the children, Mr. & Mrs. Victor Wiese, who lived in the northeast part of the county.

Metta Davis had the title of juvenile court probation officer in December 1946. The last recorded case of Metta Davis was described as "one of the strangest in police annals."

In May 1949, there were reports of a "vampire boy" who was mutilating dogs. Policewomen Betty Summers and Metta Davis learned from neighbors that a youth named David Chadwick, aged 19, may be responsible for mutilating a dog recently. They said he was crawling through the area, barking like a dog.

Investigating on the night of May 7th, the policewomen found conditions of "unbelievable filth" in three one-room shacks that the boy lived in with his parents and nine other siblings on the edge of a dump, at 2456 Dakota Street.

They found Chadwick baying like a dog in the full moonlight. They saw him chewing the throat of a small dog and sucking the blood. Upon being spotted, he dropped the dog, crouched in bushes and barked at them. The dog, bleeding from the throat and back of the neck, died an hour later.

Two male officers later spotted Chadwick, glassy eyed and incoherent. He barked at them. The officers overpowered Chadwick and manacled him hand and foot. David Chadwick was taken to the General Hospital psychiatric ward under heavy police guard, May 7, 1949. He was slightly built at 5'6", 108 pounds. Chadwick was sentenced to a year on the State Farm, May 26, 1949.

Metta Davis personnel sheet.

Sergeant James Payne of the city dog pound said rabies tests were negative on the mangled carcass of the dog that Chadwick allegedly chewed on. He was planning on pursuing animal cruelty charges pending outcome of psychological tests. Metta Davis and Betty Summers planned to go back to investigate the living conditions further on May 9th.

Metta retired from IPD on February 25, 1953, due to a severe illness. She died April 10, 1953 in Methodist Hospital. She was a member of the Queen Esther Chapter, Order of the Eastern Star, White Shrine and the Fraternal Order of Police. There were no survivors. She was cremated.

Genevieve Means was born December 2, 1896 in Brookfield, Indiana to Clarence Means and Fannie Smock. Genevieve was a graduate of Manual Training School in Indianapolis, June 1915.

She graduated from Indiana University in 1920 with a B.A. in Sociology. Genevieve had also completed course work for an M.A. in Social Work from IU. She had worked as a probation officer in charges of women's cases at the Juvenile Court, 1917-1919. She was associated with the Charity Organization Society for 9 months.

College photograph

She was appointed October 12, 1920 as a policewoman with the Indianapolis Police Department, being assigned badge number 132.

She resigned from the department on December 18, 1921, one of three women who had been told to resign because they were under the age of 30. On June 8th of that year, she wed Ralph A. McLeod. They had two children, Betty and Phillip.

After leaving city government, Genevieve McLeod worked in the Social Service Department of Indianapolis Public Schools.

Genevieve Means McLeod Scholarship was established at Indiana University in 2000 to be awarded to a female student achieving academic excellence and having a demonstrated financial need.

Genevieve died on November 9, 1988 in Indianapolis, Indiana.

28

H elen M. Franke was born 1900 in Indianapolis, Indiana to Andrew and Minnie (Zwicker) Franke. Like Genevieve McLeod, she graduated from Manual Training School. She graduated from

---

28 Official IPD portrait, 1921.

Butler University in 1921. She was a member of Delta Delta Delta Sorority. She worked as a Deputy Clerk for the Internal Revenue in 1920.

College photograph

She was appointed as a policewoman with IPD on March 2, 1921. She was forced to resign, which she did on December 18, 1921, because she was under the age of 30. She was employed by IPS, 1930.

On May16, 1933, in Indianapolis she wed
Edward J. Hughes, a dentist. They had one
child, Margaret.   Helen died February 15,
1991, Indianapolis. Buried in Crown Hill
Cemetery.

Rachel P. Bray was born December 2, 1898
in Noblesville, Hamilton County, Indiana to
Perry Bray and Elizabeth Perry. Her
family registered her birth in the Hinkle
Creek Monthly Meeting of the Quaker
Church. She grew up in Noblesville,
graduating from Noblesville High School,
1917.

Rachel was appointed to the Indianapolis Police Department as a policewoman, March 8, 1921. She was one of the four policewomen under the age of 30 who turned in their resignation under pressure, December 18, 1921.

Rachel, Noblesville H.S., 1915

However, Rachel Bray was reappointed by the Board of Safety on January 4, 1922 as a policewoman.   Rachel was very talented and apparently the board recognized that. She was assigned to the Juvenile Court.

A funny incident occurred January 6, 1923. A stray monkey was brought into the lost and found department. Policewoman Anna Brunner at the information desk told them to take it to the detective division.

There, it climbed up on a book where robberies were recorded. Detective George Sneed tried to grab him, but the monkey took a swing at him and Sneed fled to his desk. George Roach, electrician tried and the monkey jumped at him, Roach fleeing into the roll call room with the monkey chasing him.

The monkey ran into Sergeant Allison but when the monkey grabbed for him, he ran with the monkey in pursuit. It then ran into secretary to the Chief Oscar Queisser's office and saw Rachel Bray. It jumped into her lap. She petted it and the monkey became meek, allowing her to grasp his chain and put it into a chicken coop.

Rachel was working as stenographer for Chief Herman Rikhoff in January 1923.

On May 28, 1923, Rachel Bray was placed in charge of the new Accident Prevention Bureau. This was part of the Traffic Department. Rachel had been studying traffic for some time.

Rachel was a speaker along with two male traffic officers November 7, 1923 before the Parent-Teacher clubs of the public schools. The subject was "No Accident" week, something the Accident Prevention Bureau under Miss Bray had been talking about for some time.

Traffic Department – 1929. Left to right, Anna Brunner, Mame Moratz and Captain Lester Jones.

On November 9, 1923, "No Accident" week climaxed with a large parade of 1,200 school children who were participants in the safety programs at their schools. They ended up in front of the steps of City Hall, where Mayor Lew Shank gave a speech.

Standing next to the mayor was Rachel Bray, Chief Rikhoff, members of the Board of Public Safety and the City Council, as well as her supervisor Captain Michael

Glenn of the Traffic Department. This was quite an honor for this 24-year old policewoman.

Rachel Bray was promoted to the rank of Sergeant – for a week. She requested the Board of Public Safety to reduce her back to patrolwoman on January 8, 1924. She made this request after learning that Mayor Shank disapproved the promotion on the grounds that other policewomen would be dissatisfied. She told Chief Rikhoff she'd prefer remaining a policewoman than creating issues within the department.

One of Rachel's chief duties was to compile accident statistics, which she did frequently.

The Board of Public Safety promoted Policewoman Mary Moore to the rank of Sergeant on July 15, 1924. They assigned her to replace Rachel Bray in the Accident Prevention Bureau.

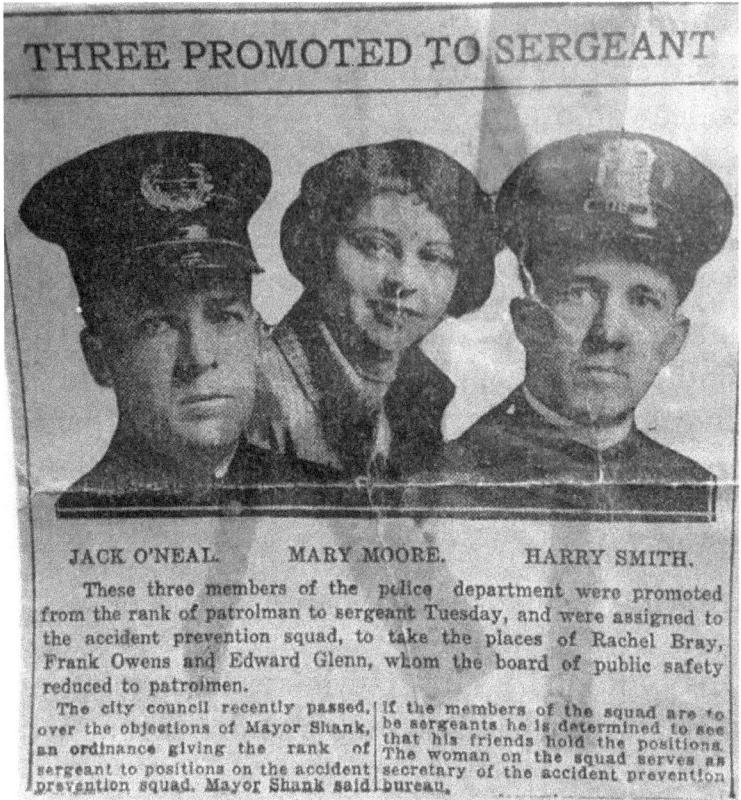

THREE PROMOTED TO SERGEANT

JACK O'NEAL.   MARY MOORE.   HARRY SMITH.

These three members of the police department were promoted from the rank of patrolman to sergeant Tuesday, and were assigned to the accident prevention squad, to take the places of Rachel Bray, Frank Owens and Edward Glenn, whom the board of public safety reduced to patrolmen.

The city council recently passed, over the objections of Mayor Shank, an ordinance giving the rank of sergeant to positions on the accident prevention squad. Mayor Shank said if the members of the squad are to be sergeants he is determined to see that his friends hold the positions. The woman on the squad serves as secretary of the accident prevention bureau.

Rachel, who the Indianapolis News described that day as "one of the most capable women in the police department", would be reassigned as assistant secretary to Chief Rikhoff. She was credited with being largely responsible for the safety programs begun in the public schools since her appointment to that bureau. She had also compiled a complete statistical record of accidents that occurred during that time.

364

Chief Rikhoff left town for Montreal, Canada, to attend the international convention of police chiefs, and in his absence, Mayor Shank ordered the transfer of Rachel Bray out of the Accident Prevention Bureau. "Because she talks too much", Shank remarked.

Bray said she would wait until the chief returned, because the Mayor had nothing to do with her position. The election of 1922 had a lot to do with this controversy. When elected mayor, Shank said that he would see that Miss Bray, who was hired in the previous administration and was not for him in the election, would not get any favors. Conversely, her replacement, Mary Moore, had supported Shank in 1922 and therefore, he was for Moore.

Chief Rikhoff protested this move. He regarded Rachel Bray as one of the most capable women in the police department and believed that her knowledge of accident prevention work would make her transfer a serious mistake.

Upon his return to Indianapolis, Chief Rikhoff refused to transfer Rachel Bray (as well as a couple of other officers). Mayor Shank said, "Rikhoff is running the department. If he wants to keep Miss Bray, Glenn and Owens in the accident prevention bureau, it is up to him. But, Miss Moore, Jack O'Neal and Harry Smith have been promoted and sergeants under the Council's ordinance, and they are still sergeants. If the chief wants to use them in the accident prevention bureau, he can, but if he wants to keep Miss Bray, Owens and Glenn, nobody can stop him, even if they are sergeants. It's up to him to find work for them to do."

On July 10, 1925, Rachel was named to the women's committee in charge of greeting the annual convention of the International Association of Chiefs of Police.

Rachel married Wilbur C. Schwier on October 18, 1925 in Indianapolis, at Trinity Lutheran Church. They left afterwards for a trip to New York. They had a son, James.

The police department was creating 16 new police districts out of the current ones in December 1925 to accommodate 55 newly appointed patrolmen. Rachel Schwier, stenographer to Chief Rikhoff, was assigned to the work of redistricting the police city.

Rachel Schwier was promoted to Sergeant on January 4, 1926. The police department created the Bureau of Missing Persons on January 16, 1926. Rachel, as sergeant in charge of policewomen, would work with Policewoman Leona Foppiano, in charge of the bureau, in finding policewomen to work in it.

On December 29, 1926, Rachel was demoted from Sergeant to policewoman because there was no provision for higher ranks for women in the 1927 budget. She was assigned as assistant to the secretary of the Chief in 1927. She was one of five policewomen the Chief of Police wanted to keep, while dismissing 15. At some point in 1927, Rachel decided to leave IPD.

On October 5, 1937, she was appointed supervisor in the old-age department of the Marion County Welfare Board.

Her husband Wilbur died on April 13, 1940. In 1941 she was the president of the Trinity Businesswoman's Club.

On July 25 1944, Rachel Schwier, formerly public assistance consultant in the Indiana State Department of Public Welfare, was named case worker. She had served four years as case work supervisor for the Governor's Commission on Employment Relief in Marion County and six years was case work supervisor for the Marion County Department of Public Welfare.

It's pretty clear that looking back from now, that Rachel Schwier lived today instead of 1924; she might have been Chief of Police of the Indianapolis Metropolitan Police Department. The same could be said of a number of the other early policewomen.

As case work director of the Lutheran Child Welfare Association, she met two Latvian refugee boys on July 10, 1947 at the airport. The boys would live at the Lutheran Children's Home.

Rachel remained very active in club work and social work.   Rachel served as resident director of Lutherwood institution for 20 years, retiring in 1962.

Rachel Schwier, left, receiving the James L. Fieser Award.

In April 1963, she earned the James L. Fieser Award from the Indianapolis Social Workers club for her outstanding work for 30 years.

She was a director of the United Fund Christmas Bureau, chapter president and regional governor of Zonta International.

Rachel Bray Schwier died in a Lebanon, Indiana, nursing home on June 15, 1986, aged 87.

Nell Wishard Dunkle was born December 25, 1883 in Indiana to Alfred Dunkle and Mary Rankin. Alfred Dunkle graduated from Hanover College and was

---

[29] Official IPD portrait from 1920.

superintendent of schools at North Vernon and later, Delphi, Indiana. He moved to Indianapolis, Indiana about 1884.

The family resided at 2010 Ruckle Street, Indianapolis, in 1900. Nell attended Shortridge High School. Alfred Dunkle sold real estate. Nell graduated from Hanover College.

Nell was involved in charity work for the unfortunate in 1908, through the North Park Christian Church.

By 1910 the family had relocated to 2727 Bellefontaine Street. Nell's father was now working in the City Controller's office. Nell was an agent for the Board of State Charities. She investigated the living conditions of orphan children living in private homes.

Nell and her sister Alice took a trip in August 1913, visiting Buffalo, Niagara Falls, Detroit and Toronto.

She continued working at the Board of State of Charities through 1920. She travelled throughout Indiana as part of her work.

Nell W. Dunkle was appointed a policewoman with the Indianapolis Police Department on September 7, 1920. She was issued badge number 103. Nell was 5'4", 130 pounds. She was one of the few Democrat policewomen on the force. Nell was promoted to the rank of Sergeant, March 8, 1921.

Nell was one of four policewomen assigned to the detective bureau when the Department of Policewomen was eliminated, January 2, 1922. She was demoted from sergeant to patrolman when this occurred.

On February 22, 1922, Nell and Policewoman Cozette Osborn were transferred by Chief Herman Rikhoff from the Detective Bureau to the Juvenile Court. They would now work for Sergeant Clara Burnside again.

The Board of Safety asked that Nell Dunkle be transferred back to the Detective Bureau, which was done on March 9, 1922. This was done because Mae Rupert was reappointed to IPD and needed a partner in the bureau. Nell joined policewomen Bertha Duclus, Irene Beyer, Sadie Osborn, and Sarah Murray there.   Much of their work was working undercover in downtown stores, looking for shoplifters.

An IPD officer named Robert Johnson was found to be guilty of trying to rape a 14-year old girl he gave a ride to. Policewoman Dunkle issued an arrest warrant from Juvenile Court for his arrest, which was done when he appeared at 11 p.m. roll call, November 9, 1923. Nell was now working in the Juvenile Court again.

Nell Dunkle's personnel sheet.

Nell and Anna Brunner were partners while doing Dance Matron duties on Saturday nights, March, 1924.

She was one of the four Juvenile Court policewomen who jointly filed suit against the City of Indianapolis for trying to eliminate their jobs, December 29, 1926.

Nell was vice-president of the Indianapolis Social Workers' Club in 1928. Nell gave a talk at the meeting of the Alpha Latroian Club on "The Work of the Juvenile Court", February 16, 1930.

The police department promoted Nell to matron, December 29, 1931. She would now work in the city jail.

Nell served as Investigator for the Children's Home from February to April of 1936. This was separate from her duties at IPD. Nell was also a member of the board of the Children's Guardians of Marion County at this time. The police department downgraded her to Third Grade Patrolman, October 18, 1932.

Sergeant Charles Weddle & Nell Dunkle

Policewoman Nell Dunkle next appears as the new assistant to Sergeant Charles E. Weddle when IPD formed a new office, the Crime Prevention Bureau, March 22, 1938. They worked out of an office on the second floor of police headquarters.

Nell resigned from IPD on January 3, 1939. She was 55 years old when she married five days later to John C. Geckler. John C. Geckler served as judge of the Juvenile

Court from 1930 to 1938 and had earlier
served as City Clerk.

New Policewomen Receive Badges

Nell Geckler is standing, 3rd from left.

During World War II, IPD suffered a severe
manpower shortage due to all the policemen
joining the service. The department
appointed 10 policewomen to meet the
emergency. One of them appointed on May
4, 1943 was Nell Dunkle Geckler.

The women received their badges in the
office of the Board of Safety, with Mayor
Robert H. Tyndall and Chief of Police
Clifford F. Beeker seated at the table. The
women were appointed to combat the
juvenile delinquency problem then going on
in Indianapolis. Nell was issued badge
number 23.

Nell's husband John died on July 8, 1945 at age 76, at their home at 3419 North Pennsylvania Street. Nell resigned from the Indianapolis Police Department on November 25, 1945. She was then 61 and with the war over, IPD expected the policewomen to resign.

Nell lived a quiet life until January 17, 1975, when she passed away in Indianapolis. A former member of the Sutherland Avenue Presbyterian Church, Nell was buried in Crown Hill Cemetery.

Mayme E. Pettiford was born April 16, 1872 in Franklin, Indiana to John and Sarah (Valentine) Pettiford. John W. Pettiford was born in Vincennes, Illinois. An African-American, he married Sarah Valentine in Indianapolis, 1862.

John Pettiford settled in Franklin, Indiana in 1863, opening up a barber shop. Mayme lived here in 1880 with her parents. Mayme wed James N. Shelton on November 28, 1894 in Franklin. They had a daughter,

Zelda, born in 1898.   They moved to Indianapolis in 1899 and bought a home in the 500 block of California Street on the west side.

On December 3, 1912 and April 14, 1914, the National Association of Colored Women's Clubs (NACWC) met at Mayme Shelton's home on California Street. Another member of this group at this time was Hettie Brewer. Both women would become Indianapolis policewomen in 1922.

Mayme was on the reception committee for the state meeting of the NACWC organization to be held September 1, 1914. Mayme was also a longtime member of The Women's Club, the oldest club for African-American women in Indianapolis. They met regularly at Mayme's home

James, Mayme's husband, was a prominent owner of a funeral parlor located at 418-420 Indiana Avenue, as early as 1915.

That year, their daughter Zelda Mariam Shelton enrolled in Fisk University, Nashville, Tennessee. Her father James Shelton died on June 7, 1921 of uremia.

When Lew Shank became Mayor in 1921, he had the police department get a number of policewomen to resign, while hiring 14 new ones. Widowed and needing to make a living, Mayme Shelton was one of the new ones, who were appointed January 2, 1922.

Mayme was assigned to patrol the African-American neighborhoods with another new policewoman, Hettie Brewer. Mayme was assigned badge number 424, was 5'3" and weighed 130 pounds.

Mayme Shelton has the distinction of being the first policewoman who used her revolver on the job. On May 22, 1922, Mayme was returning to her district in the afternoon after guarding children at a schoolhouse on the northwest part of town.

She saw a youth running west on North Street and heard several pursuers yelling "Stop thief." Mayme, who was walking south to California Street, joined in the chase and fired one shot in the air. The youth stopped upon hearing the shot.

At police headquarters, the youth gave his name as Nathaniel Freeman. He was charged with stealing a watch. He was fined $5 and costs on a charge of petit larceny in city court.

Mayme resided at 516 North California Street, 1922. On October 9th she patrolled her district. She became ill that evening and died at 10 p.m. of a stroke.

POLICEWOMAN DEAD

"Mrs. Mayme Shelton was on duty Monday and patrolled the district to which she had been assigned. She was taken ill suddenly Monday night number and died in a short time."

Mayme was the first policewoman to die while serving on the Indianapolis Police Department. She was buried in Crown Hill Cemetery.

Mayme Shelton personnel sheet.

Mayme's daughter Zelda M. Shelton moved to New York and began landing roles in five Broadway productions between 1937 and 1944, including two revivals of "Porgy and Bess".

Elizabeth M. Dean was born March 1, 1877 Grant County, Indiana to James H. Dean and Sarah Jordan. The family moved to Osage County, Kansas, where they were living in 1880. Lizzie Dean was three years old in that census. Her father was working as a blacksmith.

Elizabeth married Orville M. Denny on September 16, 1908 in Indianapolis, Indiana. The couple lived at 1513 East 17th Street in 1910. Orville was a barber.

Elizabeth was appointed a policewoman with the Indianapolis Police Department on January 3, 1922, along with 13 other women. She had served on a committee in December 1921 to design a uniform for the policewomen. She was hired with the rank of sergeant and assigned to the Humane Department. She was reduced to the rank of policewoman on March 1, 1922.

Elizabeth Denny was reassigned from Matron to the Uniform Division on September 27, 1922 by Chief Herman Rikhoff. She was to patrol districts. Her replacement was Irene Beyer.

The removal of Elizabeth Denny as matron brought about much umbrage with the Garfield Civic League. They held a meeting the evening of October 1, 1922 which resulted in a committee of seven women being appointed to investigate the police department and try and get Elizabeth Denny reinstated as matron of the city jail.

Chief Herman Rikhoff stated that this was extremely unfair. He further said that "no seven women who have had no experience in police work and who are not acquainted with conditions as they exist in the police department are going to come down here and tell me what to do."

He explained that Mrs. Denny was removed from her position as matron after receiving complaints about the matron's office from a police captain.

Rikhoff read off the list of complaints, which included Elizabeth Denny being found asleep on a cot in a room next to the matron's office. She was also found eating ice cream with her husband in that room. On another occasion, Denny was sitting in a rear room of the office while a man was talking to a woman prisoner at the jail door, out of Denny's sight. Denny was warned each time.

The Garfield Civic League met again the night of October 12th. They demanded that radical changes be made in how the city did business. They made a resolution asking that Mayor Shank remove the police department from politics and asked that the police department's management be investigated. Meanwhile, Elizabeth Denny was working out of the City Controller's office as a license fee investigator.

Events took another turn when Sergeant Clara Burnside turned in her resignation, effective October 31, 1922. On that day, the Board of Public Safety promoted Elizabeth Denny to the rank of Sergeant, replacing Burnside.

The mayor of Indianapolis was out of town when he heard of the uproar over Elizabeth Denny's transfer and was upset about it.

It was known that Mayor Shank had sent Chief Rikhoff a letter instructing him to promote Elizabeth Denny, so this was seen as another example of the Mayor going over the chief's head.

At the recommendation of Chief Rikhoff, the Board of Safety demoted Elizabeth to patrolman on January 11, 1923. They reassigned her as Matron of the City Court. Elizabeth had stated when transferred to the Juvenile Court several weeks earlier that she wanted to stay in the matron's office.

While inspecting the women's cells on June 25, 1924, Matron Elizabeth Denny discovered the body of inmate Helen Humphrey, 36. She had hanged herself in her cell. Elizabeth was still a matron in late 1926.

Elizabeth was walking a beat in Garfield Park on June 16, 1932. While on an errand, Lieutenant Owen, her supervisor, not finding her, reported her absent without leave. She explained that she had tried to call in as required at a Gamewell call box but had to wait over 30 minutes to make that call. She was suspended June 17th.

On August 30, 1932, Elizabeth Denny told the Board of Safety she had left the park to pay her union dues at police headquarters. She considered that reporting for duty. She was dismissed that day from IPD, along with Margaret Hildebrand, who had also been suspended June 17th for a similar absence.

Elizabeth died in the hospital, October 8, 1944 of a stroke. She was buried in Washington Park East Cemetery. Her husband Orville died only a month later, November 6, 1944.

Irma Leland Goff was born February 27,
1887, in Vernon, Indiana to Herbert Goff
and Sarah Fisher. In 1900, the family lived
on Washington Street in the town of
Vernon, in Jennings County. Herbert Goff
owned a flour mill.

Coming to Indianapolis, she married
Stanley C. Byrum on December 26, 1906.
In 1920 they resided at 1827 Ruckle Street.
They had three children, Bertha, Mildred
and Irma. Stanley was a salesman at a
flour mill.

During the mayoral election primary of March, 1917, Lew Shank, defeated candidate for the Republican nomination, said he was defrauded of the nomination.

He claimed there was a vast amount of fraudulent, false and felonious voting involved. He had ten investigators getting 1,500 affidavits alleging fraud. These were placed in complaint he filed with Judge Joseph R. Roach in Superior Court. One of the investigators was Irma Byrum.

Irma was appointed a census enumerator on December 27, 1919 for District 56. She was appointed City Chairman of the women members of the Shank for Mayor Club, August 16, 1921. In December, she served as chairman of the committee to design a new uniform for policewomen.

Irma was employed as a stenographer/clerk when she was appointed a policewoman with IPD, January 2, 1922. Her first assignment was to assist Robert R. Sloan, city market master, to clean up the aisles of the market and investigate sanitary conditions of the market. Also assisting was Policewoman Mary Moriarty.

Policewoman Irma Byrum

On July 10, 1925, Irma was named to the women's committee in charge of greeting annual convention of the International Association of Chiefs of Police.

Irma resigned from the police force in 1926. She took a job as secretary of the church school of the Memorial Presbyterian Church.

Irma died in a nursing home, February 13, 1975 in Indianapolis. She had been a member of Memorial United Presbyterian Church. She was survived by daughters Bertha J. Frye, Mildred Featherston and Irma J. DeMott. Irma is buried in Crown Hill Cemetery.

Sarah May Denson was born August 18, 1889 in Chillicothe, Ross County, Ohio to John A. Denson and Anna Abbott. In 1899, Anna remarried to Richard Cross, an Indianapolis poultry dealer. They lived at 316 North Pine Street that year.

They Were Wed in Old Kentucky.

JAMES E. MURRAY.   MRS. SARAH DENSON MURRAY.

Blocked by the refusal of the young woman's parents James E. Murray and Miss Sarah Denson eloped to Louisville, were married and are now at home at 611 North New Jersey street.

Sarah Denson married June 18, 1906 in Louisville, Kentucky to James G. Murray. In 1920, he was a salesman for a coal company and Sarah was comptroller for an automobile factory. They lived at 1703 East Michigan Street, Indianapolis. Sarah filed for divorce from her husband on July 16, 1921.

Sarah Murray had done office work prior to being appointed to the Indianapolis Police Department, September 13, 1921. She was issued badge number 460. Sarah was probably the smallest officer on the police force at 5'1", 97 pounds.

Sarah was assigned to the Detective Bureau on January 2, 1922. She and Sadie Osborne made an unprecedented arrest by driving without male escort to Richmond, Indiana on January 25, 1922 to arrest a man for contributing to the delinquency of a young girl. Richmond police were reportedly surprised when they saw women, not men, arrive.

Sarah Rogers, "woman detective", sat in while a female witness gave a statement to homicide detectives investigating a murder, on November 23, 1922. She used the name Rogers from this point on.

Sarah's job was eliminated on December 29, 1926 along with 14 other policewomen. She filed a lawsuit against the city to prevent this, as did four other policewomen. This brought about an injunction.

Sarah Murray personnel sheet.

She worked for 5 months without pay in 1927 before resigning in early May 1927. She was last known to be living in Los Angeles, California in 1954.

30

Mary Zoller was born 1890 in Indianapolis, Indiana to John and Mary Josephine Schmidt. John A. Zoller was born in Switzerland and came to Indianapolis in 1877. His first job was as

---

coachman to Conrad Baker, governor of Indiana. He spent 50 years working for the Pennsylvania Railroad as a car inspector.

In 1910 the Zoller's lived at 2304 Bluff Road. That year, Mary was working in a factory. Mary wed Patrick "John" Moriarty on October 16, 1912 in Indianapolis.

The Bluff Road (Ind. 37) southwest of Indianapolis and a large surrounding area were inundated by flood waters from nearby White River in 1913. The plant of the Frank Hilgemeier & Brother Packing Company (left) and the large home of Mrs. Mary Zoller (right) were inaccessible. The B'Nai Torah Cemetery now occupies ground where the Zoller house stood. Picture lent by Mrs. Zoller's daughter, Mrs. Mary Moriarity (a retired policewoman), 2425 Shelby Street, Indianapolis.

The Great Flood of March 1913 inundated the area around the Zoller family home.

John Moriarty became an IPD officer in 1921. Mary was involved in the electoral campaign 1921, being appointed ward committeewoman of the Thirteenth Ward of the Women's Department of the Shank for Mayor Club, August 24, 1921.

Her loyalty was repaid as Mary was appointed a policewoman with IPD on January 2, 1922. She was issued badge number 412. Her job would be to be assistant to the City Market Master.

Mary was on duty at the City Market, March 7, 1925 when she saw Herbert Johnson try to steal a woman's purse. She arrested him. He was found guilty and sentenced to 40 days on the State Farm.

Mary was part of a women's fund raising group which raise $295.50 as part of a city-wide effort trying to raise $683,000 for the Indianapolis Community Fund, November 1926. She was part of this effort in November 1927 also.

SOUTH DIVISION WOMAN'S GROUP LEADS COMMUNITY FUND WORK

The south division of the woman's army of the Community Fund is setting the pace for the other three divisions in this group. Among the district chairmen who are well along in the race are: (Left to right) Miss Magdalene Eberhardt, Mrs. Pauline McKay, Mrs. George J. Yoke and Mrs. Patrick Moriarity.

From the November 1927 fundraising effort.

Mary survived the "purges" of 1926 and 1932. She was walking in the 400 block of Minnesota Street on June 16, 1933 at night, when she was followed by a suspicious man. She fired her revolver and the man fled. Police caught him and charged him with vagrancy.

Mary Moriarty Personnel sheet

Mary was assigned to the Registration Office at police headquarters in 1940. She was transferred to the Juvenile Aid Division in 1941. She retired in September 1948 after 26 years with IPD.

Mary died on May 31, 1970 in Indianapolis. She was buried in St. Joseph Cemetery.

Cozette Catherine "Cozy" Case was born April 22, 1891 in Indianapolis, Indiana to Joseph Case and Anna Feltz. The Case family lived at 1260 Ringgold Street in Indianapolis, 1900. Joseph Case sold meat on a cart. He later was a deputy sheriff. His father had served as sheriff of Franklin County, Indiana.

Cozette married on October 23, 1909 to Harry W. Osborn in Indianapolis, Indiana. They had a son, Melvin Osborn (1912-1997). Cozette graduated with honors from the Benjamin Harrison School of Law. She was a member of Alpha Phi Omega sorority. She also attended business college and became an expert typist and steno typist.

Cozette was one of the policewomen appointed by the Board of Safety with the advent of the Mayor Lew Shank administration, on January 2, 1922.

She was issued badge number 414 and was one of four policewomen assigned on her first day to the Detective Bureau. On April 14, 1922, Cozette was assigned to patrol the Traction and Terminal Station.

Policewoman Cozette Osborn found dance hall regulations being violated at 903 Ketcham Street on April 26, 1924. She filed a report that said children 10 to 12 years of age were admitted and there was no Dance Matron on duty.

Top: Mary Kinder. Bottom, Harry Pierpont

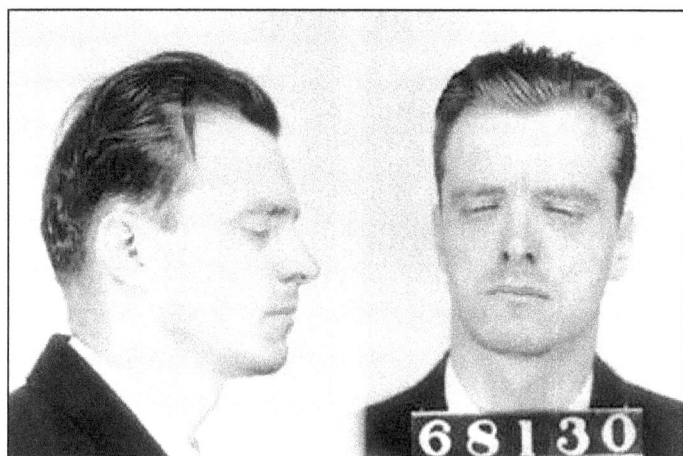

During the John Dillinger gang era, she brought back the gun moll friends of the gang, such as Mary Kinder, an Indianapolis native who was Harry Pierpont's girlfriend.

Realtor Bert F. Callahan was found slain April 6, 1934 in one of the most sensational murder cases in Indianapolis history. He was found dead on the floor of his apartment at 1636 North Illinois Street, with a bullet in his head. A woman dressed in white was seen on the front porch at midnight, a few hours before his body was found.

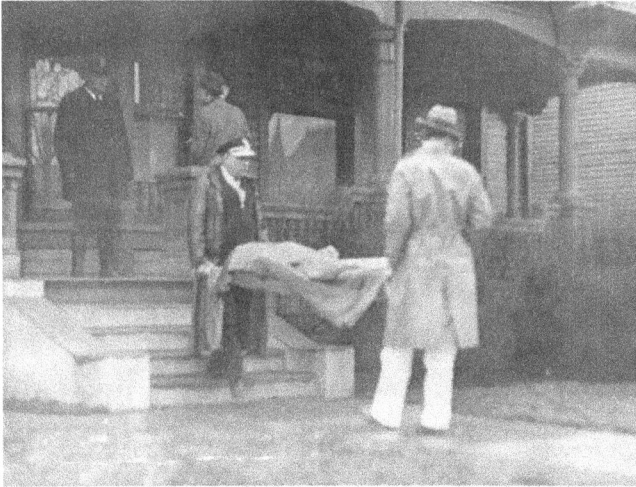

IPD officers remove the body of Bert Callahan, murder victim.
April 6, 1934 Wire photo.

3-YEAR POLICE HUNT ENDS

CHARLES STREETON   MRS. THEO SHERMAN

A Mrs. Theo Sherman, age 38, was arrested
in Cincinnati in connection with this case in
November 1934. She denied the allegation
but admitted to having a date with him a
short time before his death. She was
planning on seeking financial aid from him.

When Indianapolis police were notified,
they dispatched Lieutenant Michael Hines,
Detective Lawrence McCarty and
Policewoman Cozette Osborn to Cincinnati
to take her into custody. They were
expected back in Indianapolis the night of
November 15, 1934.

Theo Sherman told Indianapolis homicide detectives that a man named Charles Streeton confessed to the murder that night. He was finally located in San Francisco, August 1937 and returned to Indianapolis. He was sentenced to 1 to 10 years for manslaughter in this case, October 28, 1938.

In 1935 Cozette was serving as secretary in the detective department.

Cozette Osborn tripped and fell on a stairway leading to the Identification Bureau on July 16, 1938. She broke her left arm. She was given first aid by a police emergency squad and taken to City Hospital.

By 1940, Cozette had remarried to Harry J. Root. They remained married until his death.

One of the more important cases Cozette worked on occurred on August 20, 1943. A 15-year old girl from Niagara Falls, N.Y. who had been reported July 2nd to IPD, as a missing person, had been spotted by Patrolman Edward Clark as a patient at Isolation Hospital.

Policewomen Osborn and Garnet Williams were sent to talk to the girl. She said a man named Lester Price had brought her to Indianapolis and had sexual relations with her at a downtown hotel.

Osborn and Williams, unarmed and in the company of an emergency policeman named Amos Bear, with two weeks on the force, went to an east Walnut Street rooming house. There, they dragged Price out of a dark room on the Mann act. They slated him for vagrancy with a $3,000 bond.

LESTER PRICE

This was reduced to $1,000 by Judge Frank Symmes and Price was released on bond. After a while, New York police, who initially showed no interest in Price, asked IPD to hold him because his alias was Victor Cotting and was wanted by the FBI, the police of many cities and had a lengthy criminal record here and in Canada.

Price had already left town when New York requested a hold on him. Fortunately, on October 27, 1943, he broke into the offices of the school board and was arrested after a struggle with IPD officers Alexander Dunwoody and Charles Schaubhut.

She was described at her death as the first policewoman to be assigned to a police car. It was car 13, which covered the Broad Ripple area. This was during WWII.

Sergeant Clarence Lacefield

Cozette Osborn and Policewoman Nell Nutt, along with Sergeant Clarence Lacefield, went to an address on east North Street on June 27, 1945 as part of an investigation into a series of auto thefts. They arrested a 17-year old boy and a 15-year old boy.

Between them they had been involved in the theft of eight cars. The younger boy had escaped from a correctional institution and had been hiding in the weeds.

Indianapolis was experiencing a wave of criminal violence in the summer of 1945. One assault of a man in University Park was solved September 15, 1945 with the arrest of William Cody, 19, a parolee from the Indiana Reformatory. He and a 17-year old youth admitted to the crime. Policewoman Cozette Osborn and Patrolmen Earl Booth and John Haine made this case.

L-R: Mel Osborn & Denzel Poindexter, May 1, 1949.

Cozette was working out of the Juvenile Aid Division in 1945-47. One case she was involved in as that of a 17-year old who confessed on November 28, 1947 to committing 22 burglaries since escaping from the State Penal Farm on November 3rd. Taking the confession were Detective Sergeants Charles Haine and John Kestler and Cozette Osborn.

Cozette was guest speaker at the Hayward-Barcus Unit, American Legion Auxiliary on March 10, 1948. She spoke about her experiences as a policewoman for 25 years. It was held in the West Room of the World War Memorial.

Cozette turned in her badge to Chief Edward Rouls on July 1, 1949, retiring from IPD after 27 years. The chief allowed newsmen in to take her photo for what was the first time during her career.

On why she joined the force, she said "I had two husky sons and my mother to support." She said that in 1922, the department frowned on policewomen and showed no partiality to her. She asked for no favors. Cozette worked the longest hours and toughest patrol beats.

She spent time in these areas; detective homicide, vice and narcotics squads and served on downtown details picking up shoplifters and pickpockets, some of whom were nationally known. Cozette of course also worked for the Juvenile Aid Division.

"I've never had to call for help. I just went after my man and I got him. I've never shot anyone because I've never used my .32 pistol, although I took target practice to learn to use it."

During her time on the force, Cozette Osborn travelled to 28 states, to retrieve prisoners for IPD. She assisted in many police raids.

One story police officers recall about "Cozy" was when she and a rookie patrolman trailed a man into a cheap rooming house. When they walked in they were facing a "big bruiser" who refused to be arrested by policemen or women.

The rookie ran out for help, leaving Cozette to handle the man. By the time a police squad arrived, she had the situation well in hand, the "brute" being pretty messed up by now. He meekly followed policemen to the jail.

Her son Melvin Osborn was serving IPD and rose to the rank of Lieutenant before his own retirement. He served from 1946-1966. Her other son, Norbert, was a business representative for the electrical workers' union.

She was looking forward to retiring to a newly built home on U.S. 40 near the town of Greenfield, Indiana. It sat on a hill, overlooking eight acres of land. "And I'm not going to raise chickens. I'm just going to sit around and dream about my police work. I have only pleasant memories."

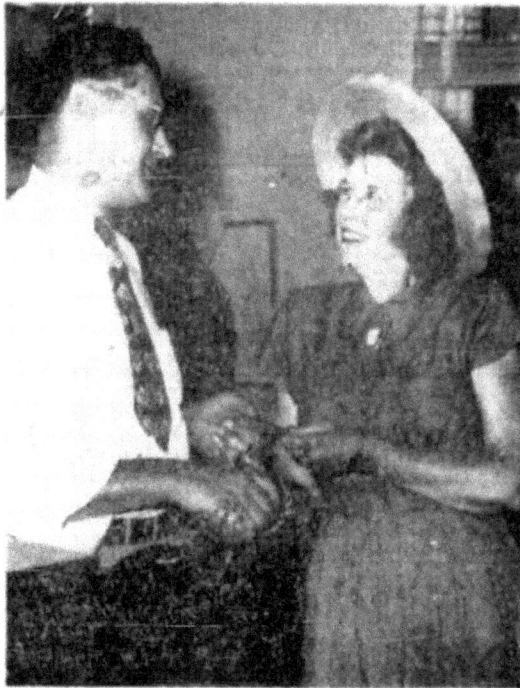

Cozette Osborn hands her badge to Chief Rouls

During her career, Cozette Osborn was a charter member of the Fraternal Order of Police and she served three terms as a trustee of the FOP.

Cozette was sought after as a speaker after retirement. She was an accomplished lecturer. Her talks about her days as a policewoman were very interesting.

This is one quote from a 1962 lecture:

"Yes, women are every bit the equal of men! What our policewomen need is to work on the street with the patrolmen like we did. That's where you learn the police business! Before radios, we handled whatever came along. Today women call for help."

She was elected secretary-treasurer of the Retired Police Officers Organization of Indianapolis, October 15, 1953. She drew on her experience as the only policewoman to have served on the board of directors of the Police Credit Union.

She took a three-week tour of Alaska in September, 1964. She avoided the city of Anchorage and areas devastated by the recent earthquake. "There were places I wanted to see and I didn't want to be bothered with a regular tour. She flew there by jet but returned by boat, train and bus, visiting friends in Olympic,

Washington, Salem, Oregon and Billings, Montana.

She served as co-chairman for an April 30, 1967 luncheon honoring Richard G. Lugar, candidate for the Republican nomination for mayor. During a trip to Europe that November, Cozette was very interested in the work done by policewomen in the countries she visited. "Like policewomen here and in other cities, they draw the same salaries as male members."

Cozette passed away in an Indianapolis retirement home, January 13, 1971. She is buried in Washington Park East Cemetery.

31

Mary Margaret Townsley was born
February 5, 1897 in Indianapolis, Indiana to
Oliver H. Townsley and Maude Manefee. In
1900, Maude and daughter Mary were
living with Maude's parents, James and
Mary Manefee, at 1214 Polk Street in
Indianapolis.

Maude (Manefee) Allman was prominent in
fraternal organizations, being past present
of the George H. Thomas Auxiliary of the

---

[31] Photograph courtesy of J.T. Williams.

G.A.R. and a member of several other groups.

Maude and Oliver Townsley apparently divorced and in 1910, Maude had remarried to Theodore Allman, a baker, and was living in Sugar Creek Township of Boone County, Indiana, to the northwest of Indianapolis.

Mary married on May 2, 1917 to Edward F. Moore in Hendricks County, Indiana. Both were living in Brownsburg, a town in that county, at the time.

Mary Moore resided at 2537 Southeastern Avenue in 1920 when she served as Republican precinct committeewoman of the Third precinct of the Tenth Ward.

Mary was an ardent supporter of Lew Shank when he ran for mayor of Indianapolis in 1921. She served on the committee appointed by Shank in December 1921 to design a uniform for IPD policewomen. She was rewarded by being appointed a policewoman on January 3, 1922. She was appointed a sergeant in the humane department that same day.

Her husband Edward Francis Moore also was appointed to the Indianapolis Police Department in 1922. He was promoted to sergeant of detectives in 1926, and then was moved to the traffic division. He was promoted to lieutenant in the detective division in 1937. Edward F. Moore retired in 1954 and passed away in 1960. He and Mary had two daughters.

Mary Moore was reduced to the rank of policewoman on January 25, 1922. She was then assigned to patrol the Traction Terminal Station. When IPD assigned policewomen to direct traffic on March 16, 1922 at area schools, Mary was assigned to St. Joan of Arc school at 42nd and Park.

An *Indianapolis Star* reporter interviewed her during a brief break. "This really doesn't rattle me at all. I'm used to traffic. I have driven an automobile for three years and the stripping of gears doesn't frighten me."

Explaining her duties, Policewoman Moore said, "I stand here in the middle of the street, not because I must but because I think it's safer until the children learn how to cross the streets properly. Then I will take up my stand on the curbing."

The children tried to walk into the street to take a look at the shining star pinned to her coat but she told them to get back. "No jay-walking there."

Mary was later sent to work out of the Juvenile Court. She did this until August 25, 1922, when she was ordered to report to Captain Edward Schubert. Mary was to patrol a district on the east side of town. She found some action within days. On August 29th she was walking east on Washington Street when she heard cries of "Stop, thief", coming from the store of Sam Epstein, 439 East Washington Street.

She looked around and saw a man running from the store and Epstein, with a pair of shoes in both hands, in pursuit. Policewoman Moore joined in the chase. She took a short cut between the buildings and cut off the suspect in an alley between East and New Jersey Streets.

The suspect threatened to attack Mary Moore as she approached him. She drew her revolver and ordered told him he was under arrest. He obeyed and was sent to the police station in a patrol wagon.

Sam Epstein said the man had started to run out of the store with two pairs of shoes, but that he jerked the shoes away from him.

Mary was removed from street patrol duty along with the other policewomen on October 12, 1922. She was assigned instead to work in the City Controller's Office, collecting delinquent license fees.

Mary Moore was transferred from the Controller's office on May 26, 1923 to police headquarters. She was expected to take the place of Rachel Bray as Chief Rikhoff's stenographer.

The board of Safety on July 15, 1924, acted on a recommendation to them from Mayor Shank and promoted Mary Moore to the rank of sergeant. Although Chief Rikhoff, who was out of town, protested, Shank said that "she was for me during the 1921 election and therefore, I am for her (Moore)." Moore replaced Rachel Bray as head of the Accident Prevention Bureau. She earned $2,000 annually for this position.

Sergeant Mary Moore had occasion to personally arrest a Mary Parsons, 28, on October 20, 1924, for failing to stop after an accident. She had struck a car in which a 14-year old girl suffered a fractured rib, and then left the scene.

Another accident occurred on November 24, 1924 where a Mrs. Gladys Dean suffered a severe back injury when her car was struck and thrown 20 feet by a car driven by J.H. Sample. While police were investigating, Sample came into headquarters to report the accident to the Accident Prevention Bureau. Mary Moore detained him until the motor police came in and arrested him on charges of assault and battery and speeding. She was there through the end of 1925.

In 1926, Mary was reduced to policewoman from sergeant and in 1927, was assigned to the Missing Persons Bureau at headquarters.

On July 30, 1927, Indianapolis police and firemen participated in an annual "field day" at Broad Ripple Park. They competed in athletic events. Policewomen Mary Moriarty and Mary Moore were in charge of the arrangements, working out of an office at 221 North Alabama Street.

By October 1929, Mary Moore was again a sergeant and was back in the Accident Prevention Bureau. She arrested a man on a charge of reckless driving, after observing the accident, March 17, 1931.

She remained in the Accident Prevention Bureau until July 8, 1931, when she was transferred out and assigned to a beat downtown, 4 p.m. to midnight, with the rank of policewoman. Joining her on that beat was Anna Brunner, who had been in the traffic department office.

Mary Moore's most dangerous moment as a police officer occurred the evening of July 22, 1932. She was assigned to work at Sullivan Park. The night started out with an IPD motor squad raiding a craps game in the park. Another man accused a youth of "tipping off" the police and beat him "unmercifully", according to Policewoman Moore's report, kicking him in the head while he was on the ground.

Moore drew her weapon and displayed her badge and ordered the attacker back. He started to move away, then turned and came toward her. She fired a shot into the ground. He lunged at her, grabbed her weapon, twisted her arm and threw Moore to the ground.

The youth who was beaten fled the scene. Other men in the park ran to Mary Moore's assistance, while others called for help at a police call box.

Holding her revolver, the suspect turned and ran away. He dropped the revolver in the canal and escaped. Police squads surrounded the park.

Mary Moore went to headquarters for another weapon and to make her report to her husband, Edward Moore, who was then a clerk in the Record Room. She then returned to her post.

Mary Moore was suspended from duty after stepping into her husband's car to get out of the rain and get some lunch money from him, September 3, 1932. A superior officer saw this and claimed she was riding around in a vehicle on duty, which was against regulations.

Rather than go through a public trial before the Board of Safety, retain an attorney and subpoena witnesses, Mary rode to headquarters on September 4th with her husband. She turned her badge into Captain Jesse McMurtry, ending a 10- year career.

Edward F. Moore, husband of Mary

32 IMPD Lichtenberger History Room.

Policewoman Yields Badge After Clash

Mrs. Mary Moore Charged With Covering Beat by Auto.

Mrs. Mary Moore, policewoman, today threw her badge on the desk of Captain Jesse McMurtry and walked out of his office, the aftermath of a clash with Lieutenant Ralph Dean, who reported she was covering her north side district in an automobile, which is against department regulations.

Dean said he found Mrs. Moore at Thirty-fourth and Illinois streets shortly after she pulled a box four blocks south on Illinois street. She was standing at the corner with her husband Edward Moore, patrolman assigned to office duty.

"What are you doing?" Dean says he asked the woman officer.

"Working," was the reply.

Dean then questioned her about covering her beat by auto. He asked Mrs. Moore to enter the police car he was using and "go down and see the captain."

Mrs. Moore

She refused, declaring, "I have my own transportation."

Later at McMurtry's office, she surrendered her badge.

Chief Mike Morrissey suspended Mrs. Moore, pending safety board trial on charges of insubordination and conduct unbecoming an officer.

Mrs. Moore said she had been distributing notices to merchants in her district that a permit is required for electric signs which hang over sidewalks, as other patrolmen have been doing the last few days.

Women officers are not popular with the present police department administration. Two were dismissed recently.

---

[33] IMPD Lichtenberger History Room. September 3, 1932.

Mary was credited with conceiving the schoolboy safety patrol program while assigned to the Accident Prevention Bureau and helping to spread it throughout the United States and England.

L-R: Detective Sergeants Claude White and George Sneed.

The man who assaulted Mary Moore was charged on September 7, 1932 with charges of robbery, grand larceny and drawing deadly weapons. Robert Breckenridge, age 23, confessed to IPD Detective Sergeants George Sneed and Claude White. He was sentenced to one to ten years at the Indiana State Reformatory on October 25, 1932 for this assault.

Mary died March 30, 1992 at her home in Fishers, Indiana, aged 95. She was a member of the Newman Mothers Club at Butler University. She was buried in Washington Park East Cemetery.

Ora Anna Secrest was born July 11, 1880 in Martinsville, Clark County, Illinois to Sanford P. Secrest and Belle Young. She married May 3, 1900 in Terre Haute, Vigo County, Indiana to Julius Brunner. The couple resided in Terre Haute that year after marriage, at 626 Locust Street. A German immigrant, Julius Brunner was a wholesale liquor seller.

In 1910, the couple resided in Terre Haute. Julius owned a grocery and saloon. They were still in Terre Haute, 1920. Anna was working as a seamstress. Anna's father Sanford P. Secrest had been living in Indianapolis since 1900, so this is why she moved there herself in 1921. She said later in life that she joined IPD after the death of her husband.

Anna was a member of the committee to design a uniform for IPD policewomen in December 1921. She became a policewoman after being appointed January 3, 1922. She was issued badge number 415. Anna was given the rank of sergeant and assigned to the Humane Department. Anna was reduced to policewoman, March 1, 1922.

On August 25, 1922, Anna was transferred from the Juvenile Court to working the information desk at headquarters. She was there through February 1924.

Anna filed a report to Chief Herman Rikhoff on March 25, 1924 that improper dancing is the rule in Indianapolis and that she, the only officer assigned as a "Dance Matron" during the week, needs more help. She was in charge of Dance Matrons in 1924.

Anna was a jail matron late in 1926. By July 1928, she was working out of the Juvenile Court. On July 8, 1931, newly appointed Chief Michael Morrissey transferred Anna Brunner from a clerical job in the Traffic Department to walking a beat on Capitol Avenue, in the interests of greater efficiency.

After a year of taking less pay after a downgrade from First Grade policewoman to Fifth Grade, on December 26, 1933, Anna was upgraded to a Fourth Grade policewoman.

Anna Brunner retired on January 2, 1944, ending a 22-year career with IPD. She planned to "stay at home and take care of the house." The department held a retirement party for her at police headquarters three days earlier. She received gifts of a house coat and slippers. Chief Clifford Beeker attended. She said she had no exciting experiences in her long career.

Unfortunately, Anna did not enjoy retirement for long. She died in her home at 359 South Spencer Avenue on November 14, 1944, aged 64. She is buried in Highland Lawn Cemetery, Terre Haute, Indiana.

Lourena F. West was born February 4, 1883 in New Richmond, Ohio to John West and Mary Petticord. In 1900, the family resided in Monroe County, Ohio. John West had emigrated from Ireland in 1868. He was a farmer.

Lourena came to Indianapolis in 1906 and wed James H. Fullilove there on February 4, 1907. She was a temperance worker early in life.

Lourena was appointed as a policewoman on January 2, 1922. Issued badge number 419, she held the rank of sergeant and was assigned to the Humane Department. Her personnel record says she was in fact given the rank of Turnkey that date.

She was demoted to policewoman in March of that year. Lourena was 5'6, 170 pounds. From 1922 to about 1926, Lourena Fullilove walked a beat at night. She did it in her determination to prove that women could do police work.

On October 13, 1924 she was working as a jail matron when she found a woman in a cell who was acting strangely. She had taken five pills in an attempt to commit suicide. She was taken to the hospital in serious condition. She served as matron in 1927-1928.

Policewoman Fullilove and Mary Moore were detailed to a downtown theater on February 28, 1928. They overheard two men talking about "good licker." They arrested both for operating a blind tiger and took them to jail. Lourena was again assigned as a jail matron in January, 1931.

Between 1931 and 1946, Lourena was attached to the Juvenile Aid Division and the Juvenile Court.

Lourena was assigned to the Juvenile Aid Division when she slipped and fell on the sidewalk outside headquarters on Alabama Street, July 23, 1942. She suffered face, hip and knee injuries and was given first aid by police.

Lourena was assigned to the Juvenile Court in January 1945. She was assigned to investigate the case of a family that lived in Ravenswood. There was no sewage system in Ravenswood and she had found poor sanitation at this home. She had visited the home every two weeks from May when the father was charged with child neglect until December, when she fell and fractured her skull.

Before being injured, Lourena reported she had considerable trouble with the Biehl family. The parents had failed to carry out her orders and clean up their home. Lourena had threatened to revoke their probation for a previous child neglect conviction to force cooperation but didn't receive much cooperation.

The Biehl's had one infant who died and five other children, who had lice infestations. They were found shivering under thin blankets on a floor pallet by deputy sheriffs investigating the death of the infant.

Another case Lourena investigated was on July 18, 1945, of a family of nine young children being looked after by an 11-year old girl. The three mothers of the children were not present when Policewomen Hattie Mitchell, Mary Wheeler and Lourena Fullilove, Juvenile Court probation officer, visited. The 11-year old was cooking lunch in the kitchen.

Lourena said all of the children needed some cleaning but the 11-year old was "doing the best she knew how to look after them." Lourena saw empty beer bottles littering some of the rooms and a strong odor of escaping gas in the kitchen.

Six of the children were taken to Juvenile Court while arrangements were made to care for them and the others.

Lourena assisted Policewoman Metta Davis on the case of children being tied up and flogged, January 11, 1946, details of which are covered in Davis' biography.

Lourena Fullilove personnel sheet.

Lourena had been attached to the Juvenile Court for quite some time by now. She retired that year. Through her tireless work with juveniles, she was credited with holding many families together. She was also active in the fight against vice and prostitution.

After retirement, she moved to St. Petersburg, Florida to live. She was a member of the First Baptist Church of St. Petersburg, Florida, the F.O.P, the business and Professional Women's Club of Indianapolis.

She died September 16, 1951 at St. Vincent's Hospital, Indianapolis while on a visit with relatives there. She was buried in Washington Park East Cemetery, Indianapolis, Indiana.

Margaret Mae Vernon was born November 30, 1872 in Anderson, Indiana, to Elmon G. Vernon and Catherine A. Clark. Her parents resided in Anderson in 1880, at 687

---

[34] Official IPD portrait from 1920.

Benton Street. Her father was a coal and lime dealer at that time.

Margaret wed George W. Osborn, on September 28, 1897 in Anderson. He was an express agent and they resided Elwood, Madison County, Indiana in 1910. They had two children, Frank V. Osborn (1898-1970) and Hope Osborn Thomas (1902-1973).

On December 3, 1913, Judge Bagot of the Madison County Circuit Court appointed Margaret Osborn as a member of the County Board of Guardians. This was a position that she hadn't been seeking, but she was interested in charity work. The position was for two years.

She filed a petition in April of 1915 with the Circuit Court of Anderson, asking that the court investigate the welfare of two children. It was stated that the mother had been arrested for intoxication and she was an unfit mother.

The members of the Golden Rule Club of Elwood, Indiana, thought Margaret would make a good police matron for their town in March 1918. They wrote a letter recommending her to Mayor John Lewis.

In 1918, the family had relocated to Indianapolis, Indiana. George was a wholesale grocer and Margaret was a social services worker.

Margaret V. Osborn was appointed a policewoman along with Mae M. Rupert and Nell W. Dunkle, on September 7, 1920. She was assigned badge number 34. Later, she had badge number 131.

She was one of the policewomen who resigned as Mayor Lew Shank's administration was taking over, on January 2, 1922. Margaret was appointed a probation officer on January 4, 1926. On January 6th, she was replaced on order of the Board of Safety by Miss Laurel C. Thayer and reduced to policewoman. She was assigned as a jail matron.

Police portrait of Margaret, possibly when reappointed in 1926

In July 1932, Margaret was one of the policewomen ordered to walk a beat formerly assigned to a male officer "in the interest of greater efficiency." On July 22, 1932, Policewoman Mary Moore was walking a beat by herself in Sullivan Park and was assaulted by a man while attempting to prevent an assault.

That same night, Margaret Osborn was walking her beat at Willard Park when two groups of men from different polo teams fought, one of whom had a broken nose. Margaret was in a different part of the park at the time of the fight, which IPD motor police didn't investigate due to it being described as a "little scrap."

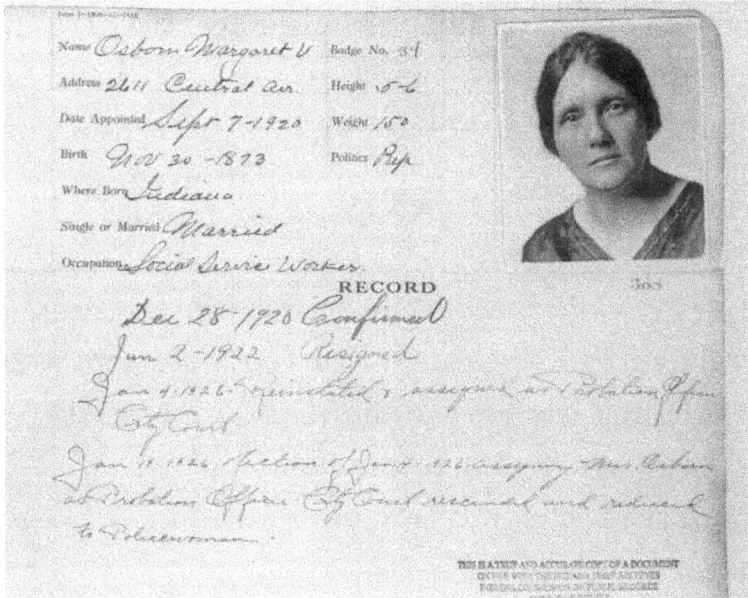

Margaret Osborn personnel sheet.

On Sunday, September 11, 1932, Margaret Osborn investigated an accident at 62nd Street and College Avenue. Finding it a routine case, without law violation or injured persons, she did not make a written report. Because she did not make a report, Chief Michael F. Morrissey suspended her on Monday. She was the fourth policewoman to be suspended in three weeks on a technicality.

As noted by *The Indianapolis News*, for some time it had been customary at IPD headquarters not to investigate a "B.F." (bent fender) accidents unless there was a law violation or a person was injured.

When a report such as this was called into the PBX operators, the operator says the only thing necessary is for the motorists to exchange license numbers and proceed on their way. Today it is much the same except for the addition of insurance information.

Chief Morrissey also filed a charge of neglect of duty against Policewoman Osborn and she was scheduled to appear before the Board of Public Safety for trial.

An editorial by the *News* on September 14th said that:

"If the police have been instructed to spy on policewomen they will be able, no doubt, to file some technical violation of the regulations on which the women can be suspended, and, when they are tried by the board of safety, they will be dismissed. Some of the civic organizations are letting the department know they are not in sympathy with such tactics and they believe policewomen, if permitted to work as they have in the past, will perform a real service for the public."

At the trial before the Board of Safety on September 27th, Silas Walker testified that he had halted his car on the street car tracks in order to stop a street car. He said a girl who was with him wanted to board the street car and this was his way of stopping it. The street car bumped his car, causing slight damage. Margaret Osborn questioned him and he took offense to her questions. He went to Chief Morrissey and made a complaint.

Margaret's testimony was that "I did not report the accident because there was nothing to report. No one was hurt. No property had been damaged." Her attorney,

Mrs. J.D. Thatcher, asked Morrissey pointed questions about whether male officers were similarly disciplined for this offense and he replied that a report should be made on each accident.

On September 28, 1932, the Board of Public Safety suspended Margaret for 60 days, retroactive to September 20th when the charges were first placed on her.

On October 5, 1932, an attorney retained by Margaret and the National Association of Working Women plead for fairness in ousters of policewomen. On October 18th, along with most of the serving policewomen, Margaret was reduced from a Second Grade Patrolman to a Fifth Grade Patrolman, making less than $1,000 a year in salary. All policewomen made $1,733 annually in 1924.

Margaret Osborn spoke on the history of policewomen in Indianapolis, on December 7, 1932, before the National Association of Working Women, at a meeting at the Hotel Lincoln in Indianapolis.

35

"Mrs. Margaret Osborn (shown in picture) will speak on probation work at the first fall meeting of the National Association of Women to be held in the Hotel Washington Monday. Mrs. Osborne is a probation officer."
(The Indianapolis News – September 21, 1934)

---

[35] Photograph courtesy of Rev. Alice J. Shirley.

Margaret was a matron in 1940. Margaret retired from IPD in 1942, having served with various bureaus within the department, including the Juvenile Aid Division.

Margaret Vernon Osborn, mother of Frank V. Osborn

Margaret died September 18, 1946 at her home on State Road 67, near Oaklandon, which was not far from Indianapolis. She was a member of the Queen Esther Chapter, O.E.S. and the Tabernacle Presbyterian Church. She is buried in the Elwood Cemetery, Elwood, Indiana.

---

[36] Photograph courtesy of Rev. Alice J. Shirley.

Laurel Conwell Thayer was born
September 27, 1873 in St. Louis, Missouri to
William W. Thayer and Maria H. Conwell.

She was named "Laurel" after the village Laurel, which was founded by her grandfather, Rev. James A. Conwell. The following details of the Thayer family come from "Thayer Quarterly"[37]

William Wild Thayer was a publisher, editor, journalist and abolitionist, born in Cambridgeport, Massachusetts in 1829. Laurel's mother Maria was a graduate from the Cincinnati College of music and was an accomplished singer. She also taught music.

After Laurel was born, the family lived in St. Paul, Minnesota (1880-1886), Seattle, Washington, Ann Arbor, Michigan and Washington D.C. In Ann Arbor, Laurel studied and taught music at the University of Michigan. At Washington D.C. she became the district executive secretary for Associated Charities of Washington, D.C. in 1907, moving there.

---

[37] Thayer Quarterly, January 2016, Volume 24, Issue 1 by Richard A. Thayer, editor.

Laurel C. Thayer - 1907

William W. Thayer was an invalid for the last 20 years of his life, being cared for by Maria and Laurel. Laurel was his biographer, typing the manuscript. They were living in Indianapolis in 1889.

Laurel was living at 138 Park Avenue in Indianapolis, 1895, attending Indiana University. Her father died in

Bloomington, Indiana, 1896, while Laurel was attending Indiana University there. She received her A.B. in Economy from the Indianapolis Teachers' College, Indiana University, 1899 and the Michigan University School of Music of Ann Arbor, Michigan.

During her father's illness, she earned money to support the family. She was a writer and a member of the press after graduation. Laurel was a teacher in 1901 and a society editor in 1902-13 in Indianapolis.

Laurel and her mother were living at 613 East 22nd Street in Indianapolis, 1910. Laurel was then a staff member of the Indianapolis Children's Aid Association. She was a member of the editorial staff of the Indianapolis Sun, 1914-1916.

Laurel was appointed matron for the City Court, on January 7, 1918. She also served as probation officer for the court. She was the first probation officer for Indianapolis. She held the rank of Sergeant in this capacity.

She was appointed to the Indianapolis
Police Department as a policewoman, on
December 28, 1921. She was demoted on
January 1, 1922 to the rank of policewoman
the Indianapolis Police Department and
assigned as probation officer in the City
Court.

Laurel Thayer official photograph

Laurel resisted this demotion, stating that
the court hired her and the police
department didn't have authority over her.
Laurel C. Thayer was reappointed City
Court probation officer on September 26,

1922 with a salary of $1,650, up from $1,100. She was still a policewoman, however.

Laurel Thayer personnel sheet.

When John L. Duvall became Mayor in January 1926, Laura C. Thayer was assigned to field duty, January 4th. She was considered by Chief Claude F. Johnson as a member of the police force and as a result, was given the rank of policewoman and assigned to duty as supervisor in dance halls in the city. Her former place as probation officer was given to Policewoman Cozette Osborn.

Laurel brought this to the Board of Safety and brought three well known attorneys with her, on January 12, 1926. They all interpreted the law to mean that her status could not legally be changed by the Board of Public Safety or by Chief of Police Claude F. Johnson. She resigned from the police department on January 20th. The Board of Safety ruled in Laurel's favor and reinstated her January 26th.

Laurel completed 9 years as probation officer for the old city court until May 16, 1927, when a new law went into effect, providing for salaried probation officers. She provided valuable lobbying to get this law passed. This ended her 5 years as an Indianapolis policewoman.

She was appointed July 23, 1927 as probation officer of Municipal Court, retroactive to May 16th, when the law went into effect.

Laurel would serve as clerk of the new probation department of the four municipal courts. She had served nine years as probation officer for the old city court.

She continued as probation officer through 1934. On December 28, 1934, she was given a letter along with the other two probation officers, that their positions were being eliminated effective January 1, 1935. They would be replaced by persons selected by the municipal court judges.
In 1943 she was employed by the Juvenile Detention Home.

Laurel C. Thayer died July 4, 1944, in
Indianapolis. She was a member of the
Society of Indiana Pioneers, National
Association of Women, Indianapolis
Teachers' College Alumnae Association and
Pi Beta Phi Sorority. She was one of the
founders of the Women's Press Club of
Indiana. She is buried with her parents in
Crown Hill Cemetery.

38

Carrie V. Wheat was born March 16, 1866 Wheeling, West Virginia to John and Sarah (Wiley) Wheat. In 1870, John J. Wheat was a sewing machine agent in Wheeling. The Wheats were living at 67 Malott Avenue, Indianapolis, in 1880. Her father was a U.S. Patent agent.

---

[38] Official IPD portrait, 1921.

Harlan P. Marshall

Carrie Wheat married on September 3, 1890 in Indianapolis to Harlan P. Marshall. They lived in Indianapolis through 1901.

She received a U.S. Patent on August 3, 1909 for inventing a marking device. Her husband Harlan died in Indianapolis, December 8, 1908, aged 42. They had two children, Edwin H. Marshall, born April 30, 1900 and Virginia Ballard Marshall, born June 8, 1901.

---

[39] Photograph courtesy of Mary Anna Wright.

In 1910, Carrie was a widow, living in Wright, Ottawa County, Michigan with her children. She returned that year to Indianapolis to take a job as a record clerk at the State Board of Charities. She was also a stenographer there.

She was appointed February 5, 1919 to the Indianapolis Police Department as a policewoman. She apparently resigned at some point as she was again appointed to IPD on January 20, 1920 as a policewoman. She worked as a stenographer there in 1920. When the Shank administration took over, she resigned January 3, 1922. She was then a jail matron.

Carrie then was employed from 1922 to 1923 as a stenographer for the Juvenile Court. She was a probation officer for the Juvenile Court from 1924 to 1930. She then retired aged 64. Surviving was her daughter Mrs. William A. Braun and her son Edwin.

Carrie Wheat Marshall

Carrie died on April 23, 1960 in a nursing home in Indianapolis, aged 94. She was

---

[40] Photograph courtesy of Chris Donn.

Name *Marshall Carrie V.*	Badge No. *Matron 73*
Address *322 Graham Av.*	Height
Date Appointed *Feb 5 – 1919.*	Weight
Birth *Mar 16 – 1866*	Politics
Where Born *West Va.*	
Single or Married *Widow*	
Occupation *Stenographic & Clerical work*	

RECORD

Jan 20 – 1920 Confirmed
Jun 2 – 1922 Resigned

buried in Crown Hill Cemetery,
Indianapolis, Indiana.

41

Verna B. Sweetman was born February 15, 1893 in Irvington, not yet incorporated into the city of Indianapolis. She was a member of a prominent family of Irvington. She was educated first at School No. 57, and then graduated from Emmerich Manual High School.

---

[41] Official IPD portrait from 1919.

After attending Butler University two years, she graduated from the University of Wisconsin in 1917. She took a position as a traveling representative of the Indiana Board of State Charities for several years.

Verna was appointed October 21, 1919 as a social worker with the Women's Bureau of the Indianapolis Police Department. Due to this, she is being included in this history although she was a civilian, not a policewoman.

She married October 20, 1920 to William W. Mendenhall, state secretary of the Y.M.C.A. She worked for the Y.M.C.A. in Indiana for 10 years, and then worked for that organization in Pittsburg, through the University of Pittsburg.

A trained organist, she played the organ 11 years at the Downey Avenue Christian Church. She died, July 17, 1939, in Pittsburg. Burial was at Memorial Park Cemetery.

Post Renaissance

During the Christmas season of 1934, Chief Michael F. Morrissey detailed a force of extra police for duty in the downtown shopping stores. This force included 38 uniformed men, 30 plain-clothes men and 12 policewomen.

He issued orders to set a "deadline" around the "Mile Square" (bounded by North, East, West and South Streets in Indianapolis). Any "police characters" as they were known, would be arrested on sight if they were within this perimeter.

This all-out effort to prevent shoplifting was repeated on December 1936 (and December 1937, 1938). Each year, 15 policewomen were among the 85 officers assigned to the downtown stores. By February 1937, the policewomen had all been upgraded to Third Grade patrolmen, making $112.50 a month.

Three policewomen were then assigned to the Record Room, which typed police reports and kept the department's records, among other duties. On January 15, 1938, IPD hired 12 civilian employees to work in the Record Room, allowing the department to reassign the policewomen to other duties.

A new office in the police department was created March 22, 1938, the Crime Prevention Bureau. Operating out of the second floor of headquarters, it was staffed by Sergeant Charles E. Weddle, his assistant Policewoman Nell Dunkle and Bertha Duclus and Emma Baker, who were assigned formerly to the Juvenile Court.

The purpose of the office was to separate juvenile law violators from adult offenders. All policemen would now bring children to the new bureau, not to Juvenile Court or the Juvenile Detention Center. This unit became known as the Juvenile Aid Division.

By September 1939, the number of policewomen in Indianapolis had dwindled down to 11, with the retirement of 21-year veteran Emma Baker the previous month. All were patrolmen's rank and doing clerical work. Veteran policemen remembered the era when Captain Clara Burnside and her "lady cops" conducted a campaign on "mashers" in the downtown district, arrested shoplifters and guarded against pickpockets.

The veteran male police felt the ladies gave a bit of refinement to the old police headquarters building, putting a rug and curtains in their room. One former female detective commented in 1939 that "There are certain kinds of police work which only a woman can perform, and I feel that we would be serving better by doing them."

The women soldiering on for the Indianapolis Police Department in 1939 were:

Cozette Osborne – Record Room
Ruth Haywood – Record Room
Leona Frankfort – Identification Bureau
Anna Yoh – Telephone switchboard
Anna Brunner – Telephone switchboard*
Margaret Osborne – Information Desk
Lillian Jaschka – Information Desk*
Mary Moriarty – Information Desk

Metta Davis – Juvenile Bureau
Bertha Duclus – Juvenile Bureau*
Lourena Fullilove – Juvenile Bureau

* One of the original policewomen

That December, for the fifth year in a row, all policewomen were called out to do shoplifting prevention work downtown. There were 20 policewomen for this duty in December 1941.

In the aftermath of the attack on Pearl Harbor, Chief Morrissey expected sabotage in Indianapolis. He believed police headquarters would be one of the first targets in an attack. Special duties were given to the 11 policewomen.

A rare bit of police work was taken up by Bertha Duclus and Mary Moriarty in June 1942. A "fortune-teller" was putting her business card on motorists' windshields. The policewomen were put on her trail and had their fortune told for $1.00 separately. They arrested the woman for fortune-telling on June 23rd.

With the drain on police manpower due to WWII, Republican candidate for mayor Robert H. Tyndall pledged to appoint more policewomen to combat the increasing juvenile delinquency in Indianapolis, which was up 85% over the past two years. By May 1943, manpower at IPD had reached a crisis point and the city appointed 55 policewomen, the first 10 receiving their badges on May 4th.

The Indianapolis Police Department made national news when they employed policewomen in May 1943, including Artie Stockdale (left) and Ann Bennett (right) who worked traffic around the Monument Circle.

Six African-American women were appointed May 11, 1943 to IPD. They were the first to join the department since January 3, 1922.

L-R: Beatrice Warfield, Georgia Rogers, Sarah Mize, Thelma Graves, Ora Phillips with their firearms instructor, Officer Jacques Durham. – September 9, 1944

Another war made policewomen viable again to the city of Indianapolis. Policewomen during WWII, like their counterparts during WWI, walked a man's beat. They carried guns in their purses and were given firearms training. They wore uniforms. At war's end, most were encouraged to resign, to make way for the 88 policemen reappointed to the department on June 16, 1946.

From 1946 to 1968, policewomen in Indianapolis were once again relegated to clerical work. They did not wear uniforms. There were some highlights.

- The recruit class appointed December 16, 1947 included eight women, who for the first time were given all the training, including in judo, that the male recruits had.
- July 15, 1953: Two African-American policewomen, Thelma Graves and Ella Coleman, are transferred from Juvenile to the Detective Division's downtown shoplift detail. This was the first time African-American women had done undercover shoplifting work since 1926.
- July 1955: Two teams of IPD officers raided the barber shop of Herman Lopez Redd, age 31 and his home at the same time. While Detective Sergeant Anthony Watkins' team raided the barber shop,

Detective Sergeant William Owen and his team, including Patrolwoman Emily C. Weathers raided the home, located at 2070 Highland Avenue. There they found Laura Redd and a supply of heroin and drug paraphernalia. During the month of July, other policewomen, all of whom were African-American, assisted on narcotics raids and a "war" on bootleg cabbies.

- 1960: There were 47 policewomen on IPD. At that time, Cincinnati and Minneapolis had 8 each.
- April 25, 1961: Policewoman Lois Peeler goes undercover as a decoy to capture three men suspected of a series of attacks on women.
- 1963: Policewomen Florence Guthrie and Ruth Bader perform all the duties of a detective in the Juvenile Branch, but would not earn that title.

- July 1967: The Indianapolis Police Department fields the first all policewoman pistol team in the United States. Left to right: Liz Coffal, Barbara Hanley, Alberta Edwards, Florence Doty. They had a good record in competition.

Finally, things began moving forward for women in 1968. Two members of the recruit class appointed April 3, 1967, Betty Blankenship and Liz Coffal, after spending time in Juvenile and Teletype, requested a transfer to street duty.

Finally, their commander Captain Edward Clouse decided to approve their request, because, as he said "it was the right thing to do." Deputy Chief Raymond Strattan and Chief of Police Winston Churchill also gave their approval.

Betty Blankenship (left) and Liz Coffal, September 1968.

Betty Blankenship and Liz Coffal were assigned to Car 47 on September 9, 1968.

They were the first in the United States to take all of the runs that male officers took.

It should be noted that Policewoman Cozette Osborn did apparently patrol in Car 13 for IPD during WWII in the Broad Ripple area but she likely did not do this without a male companion and probably did not take all radio runs.

Sergeant Paul Hooks, with Rookie Ruth Corbitt, November 1968. She was being trained on how to take reports that only male officers previously took.

In November of 1968, in a move that had been planned for months, the 20 policewomen in the recruit class that graduated in October, were put in police cars with male training partners to learn the basics of street patrol.

They took minor reports of accidents, dog bites, etc. This was so they could take jobs as dispatchers in the IPD Communications Branch and better handle these calls over the radio. However, this had never been done before and it was another step forward.

Policewomen had never served as dispatchers in Indianapolis since 1931 (and perhaps the U.S.) until women such as Gracie Layton (left) and Judy (Klein) Callahan and others did in January 1969. Gracie Layton also scored 275 out of 300 on the pistol range, best in her class, a first for a policewoman here.

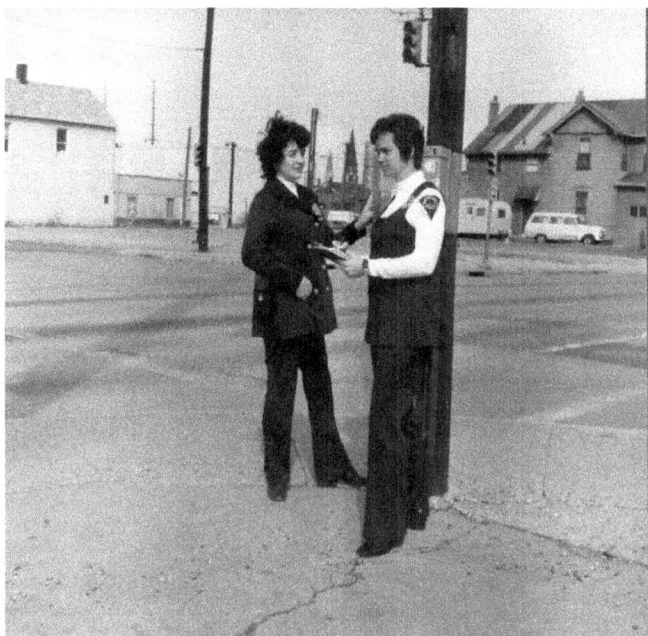

Jackie Ginther and Penny Davis, 1972

Another pair of policewomen, Penny Davis
and Jacqualine Ginther began patrolling in
the same squad car as Officers Blankenship
and Coffal, but on middle shift, in 1970.
Diana Pemberton, Jan Strattan Rahn,
Sherry Dinkins and Gracie Layton joined
them in Car 47 by 1972. Promotions also
came, but slowly. In 1972 only five
policewomen held the rank of Sergeant.

Thelma Graves, shortly after her promotion to Sergeant.

Thelma Sansbury and Thelma Graves were the first African-American women in IPD history to be promoted to Sergeant in November 1968. Sgt. Graves noted that she "always wanted to join the department since she knew of the great work Mrs. (Emma) Baker did and the kind of lady she was. 'I would call her a police lady."

Major Penny Davis

Penny Davis broke many barriers for her fellow policewomen. She was the first female sector detective, June 8, 1976. In 1980 she became the first female field supervisor for IPD.

She and Charlene Lawrence in 1981 became IPD's first female Lieutenants since the 1920's. In September 1986 she was appointed Major (another first) over a district and became the first female Deputy Chief in January 1992.

Charlene Lawrence, upon her promotion to Captain.

Charlene Lawrence became IPD's first female Captain in 1986. By now, few people remembered Clara Burnside and what she did in the 1920's.

Minority females joined the executive staff in the 1990's. Deborah Saunders was patrolling in a squad car, 1976. In 1986 she was the first African-American female to be promoted to the rank of Lieutenant.

Assistant Chief Deborah Saunders

Lt. Saunders was promoted to Deputy Chief of Downtown District in 1997 and became Assistant Chief of Support Services in January 1999. This made her the highest ranking female on the police department.

Pat Holman is appointed Deputy Chief by Chief James Toler.

Patricia Holman also made history with the police department. After promotion to Lieutenant in 1993, she was appointed Deputy Chief of North District in July 1994. She was the first African-American female Deputy Chief with IPD. Pat Holman earned a merit promotion to Captain on February 20, 2002, making her the only minority female Captain in department history.

Among the first females in the investigative division of IPD were Ruth Corbitt, Narcotics, 1970; Gaylene Weis and Elva Brakensiek, Narcotics, 1971; Peggy Patton, Sex Crimes, 1972; Jan Cotton, Narcotics,

1972; Sgt. Margaret Crouch, Donna Holmes, Norma Alvey, Alice Parnell and Jacqualyn Ginther, Shirley Olthaus, Sex Crimes, 1975; Deana McGivern, Vice, 1977; Jeanne Johnson, Judy Callahan and Gwen Black, Vice, 1978 and Donna Holmes, Homicide, 1981.

The following women were early members of IPD special services units or areas: Rene Conder & Pam Kramer, who operated the only Mobile Breathalyzer Laboratory, in the U.S., 1973; Gracie Layton, first female police firearms instructor in the U.S.; Lois Irwin, first female police helicopter observer in Indiana and possibly the U.S., 1975; Kay Cook, first rescue diver 1982; Julie Lapadat, K-9; Jeanne Johnson, Mounted Patrol, 1983 and Ann Popcheff, motorcycle officer, 1988.

Officer Teresa Hawkins was killed in an accident at East 36th Street and Emerson Avenue while she was responding to a domestic disturbance, August 17, 1993.

Her squad car was struck on the driver's side door by an intoxicated driver who ran a stop sign. She is the only female officer to

give her life in the line of duty for the
Indianapolis Police Department.

Women of the Indianapolis Metropolitan Police Department

Newly appointed interim Chief of Police for IMPD, Valerie
Cunningham (2nd from right) and other ranking female officers
of the department at a promotion ceremony, January 6, 2017.
L-R: Commander Dawn Snyder, Sgt. Christine Carver, Sgt. Ida
Williams, Sgt. Grace Sibley, Sgt. Lindsey Terry, Sgt. Tanya Terry,
Chief of Police Valerie Cunningham, Commander Karen Arnett.
Officers Carver, Sibley and Lindsey Terry were newly promoted
to the rank of Sergeant.

Notes about the cover and title page photos.

For these photos taken in 2018 by IMPD Civilian David Dickens, three currently serving IMPD police officers volunteered to model. As shown on the back cover, left to right are Sergeant Ida Williams, Patrol Officer Sonya Daggy and Patrol Officer Kimberly Kelsay.   They managed to find clothing in their closets which closely matched the uniform designed by the policewoman of the Indianapolis Police Department in 1922. They are wearing the actual six-star badge worn by IPD officers from 1918-1927.

The title page photograph depicts Sonya Daggy and Ida Williams, portraying Policewomen Mary Mays and Emma Baker. African-American, these policewomen were restricted to working in African-American neighborhoods when appointed in 1918. The scene is the famous Walker Theatre, built by Madame C.J. Walker, first African-American millionaire.   Mays and Baker would have walked this beat from 1918-1922.

www.ingramcontent.com/pod-product-compliance
Lightning Source LLC
Chambersburg PA
CBHW071400090426
42737CB00011B/1306